|= /- ! ' | ' # # /- (| < [- /2
|= 4 1 7 |- | | - | 4 (X 3 2

f417h h4ck32

Faith Hacker

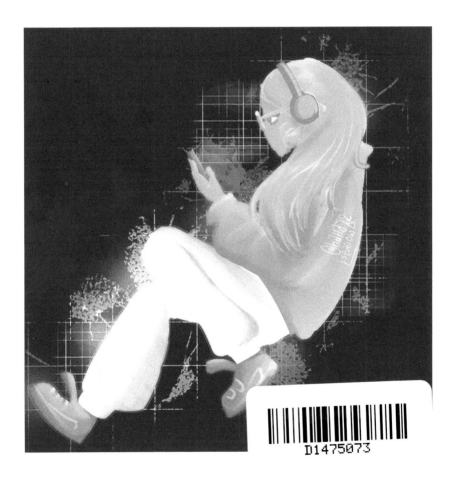

James 'Jim' Wilcox

ISBN 978-1-63814-157-0 (Paperback)
ISBN 978-1-63814-158-7 (Digital)

www.faithhackerbook.com

Cover art: "Neon!! Gorl!!!" ©2020 C. Wilcox,
(insta: [@mintytakarts](https://www.instagram.com/mintytakarts/))
Used with Permission, All Rights Reserved.

Covenant Books, Inc.
11661 Hwy 707
Murrells Inlet, SC 29576
www.covenantbooks.com

With Gratitude…

For the many who have supported and/or reviewed and/or edited along the way, including my kids, Castor Wilcox and Joshua Wilcox, and wife, Lisa, and dad, Richard.

To my church family at Movement Christian Church (#Love603)—Kristen Oser-Allen, Rich and Kristyn Mohrmann, Brett and Katie John.

To the Granite State Code Review Nightly regular hackers—Marie, Gabriel, Karen, Bob, Joe, and Andreas.

To the published Microsoft MVP authors who helped inspire the effort and provided tons of valuable tips.

Thanks to West Wind Technologies for the Markdown Monster for MVPs as well as GitHub for tools licensing.

Finally, thank you to Renee and her team of editors and publishing contributors at Covenant Books for putting up with my multiple rounds of tweaks and edits.

The views expressed in this book are from the journey of the author at a point in time, and not necessarily shared by any other person or organization or mentioned.

Contents

CHAPTER 1

Introductions

Sometime back in the 1990s...

I grew up strongly suspecting my grandfather was atheist. In my living memory, his only comments about faith, directly, had been something like, "If there is an all-knowing, all-powerful being who pays any attention to us at all, that being is probably bored to tears by people begging and groveling and sniveling."

His outward demeanor was far too stoic to reference it, but his description always reminded me of one of the comic scenes from *Monty Python and the Holy Grail*: "It's like those miserable Psalms. They're so depressing!" Maybe Grandpa saw it. Most folks would have never guessed he loved *Rowan & Martin's Laugh-In*. He was also a closet *Looney Tunes*/Bugs Bunny fan.

This time, his reaction was a surprise to me. Upon verbally observing that scripture was full of brokenness and inconsistencies, Grandpa seemed to agree.

It was almost like he'd played out this exact situation in his head. He seemed to be expecting my remarks, almost prepared for them. He grabbed a Bible off a nearby shelf. It was as if he had just put it there moments before. He put it in my hands and said, "I think you're right, but you should probably make sure." I think he knew this was a vulnerable time for me, and the moment never stops impacting me.

His wife, my gram, was a major influence in my life too. Her faith was a given, and she participated in her church and community accordingly. My sister and I spent our formative years observing her acts of community love like passengers in her car, figuratively and literally. She was an amazing example.

The Challenge

Paying forward my grandfather's challenge as best I can is what this book is about. It's about unpacking some (popularly scoffed at) tenets of Christian Scripture, from a technical engineering mindset, and letting you figure out how to debug it.

As he did, I'm intentionally withholding my assertion of any divinity. We'll talk about the divine and the sacred and the holy but only as elements relevant to the narrative. If there's a direct assertion of divinity made, I'm highlighting Scripture's claim as a matter of impact to the topic.

It's not that divinity's not important. It's that sometimes "keeping it real" brings about a hypothesis to explore. One might disagree with the physics of this or have issue with the social ramifications of that, but consider how much easier it will be to stand up to religious authority—armed with Scripture—yourself.

I'm not asking anyone to "suspend belief." I'm also trying to avoid asking anyone to "suspend disbelief." The latter is something we're asked regularly to for fantastic stories and movies, even commercial ads, all the time. I'm really just asking that we consider the scriptural stories and narratives for the value they provide without the demands of authority. Suspending belief or suspending disbelief, in both cases, is only a human problem and only when you let it be.

I was under no obligation to accept my grandfather's challenge, but I went for it. After several years, I'd read that book cover to cover like a novel and then doubled down in more focused study groups.

I'm sure I found the brokenness and inconsistencies, but they weren't at all what I thought they were.

Likewise, you are under no obligation to accept this challenge.

It's an invitation. There's no reprisal if you reject it.

A Companion

Regarding Scripture, there's plenty else of lower risk to pride to spend precious time on.

From a neighbor to you, there's an ambient psychology in Biblical scripture. Maybe that psychology is obvious to some. To others, it's a contextual element that often gets lost in the details.

Here's the core of what I'm talking about. It stands out best in the following passage:

> But when a team of socially prominent religious lawyers heard that Jesus had silenced members of another similar team, they gathered. One lawyer asked Jesus a question, testing Him: *"Teacher, which is the greatest commandment in the Law?"*
>
> And Jesus said to him, "Love the Lord your God with all you've got. This is foremost.
>
> The second builds on that, *Love your neighbor as yourself.*

> Upon these hang the whole Law and Prophets."
> (Matthew 22:34–40, emphasis and paraphrasing
> mine.)

When Jesus says "upon these hang the whole Law and Prophets," he means Scripture would be meaningless without those laws.

My hope here is to share a human journey around this topic with you

- in reading,

- discovery of the wetware platform (psychology), and

- hopefully, in discovery of a spiritual journey.

Understanding this singular evidence, there's vastly more than a tome full of stories to talk about. Much of what I'm offering are what folks call Christian "apologetics." But even there, I am writing this on the chance that there's some valuable discoveries for you in looking at the psychology of faith from a tech geek's point of view.

Who are you?

All I know for sure is that you're my neighbor. There's no doubt: You're the one this is being written for.

Maybe you're 60 percent atheist, 40 percent agnostic. Maybe you're a fellow software developer or contemporary technologist. I hope Scripture has been peripheral to you. But maybe this is an introduction to it for you.

Does Jesus really say what popular society thinks?

Does He really say what popular Christianity thinks He says?

You'll have to find your own definitive answers. But these are some points to ponder while we start to dig on them.

Maybe you're here because you're curious about different viewpoints. Maybe you're looking for a different understanding.

Who am I?

I use he/him pronouns.

I'm a husband and a dad, a brother, a son, and a grandson. I'm a computer geek, a sci-fi/fantasy geek, and a bit of a music geek.

I'm an autodidact. That is, I'm mostly self-taught. Sure. I've had plenty of formal training for various things, but I never stop learning, and that's easily been the bulk of my learning over the duration of my life.

I grew up in the rare position of knowing I was going to be a software developer since I was an early teenager. I've been at it my whole life. Dating myself, professionally, I'm coming up fast on my third decade of it, and I'm in no way slowing down.

I'm so comfortable with software development that I'm using my favorite software authoring tools (Visual Studio, in fact) to author this text with markdown. I'm even using online software version control tools (GitHub) to manage revisions and edits. This text is definitively Cloud native.

I'm also a software/tech community evangelist. I present new and practical technologies at software development networking and trade conferences. I organize trade meetups and conferences for software engineers to professionally network and invite and encourage others to be tech community evangelists too. I love to geek out about tech to help "cross-pollinate" ideas and to pay forward the opportunities I've been given.

I'm known enough for my tech evangelism in the community that Microsoft (the makers of things like the Windows OS, the Xbox game console, Office [Word, Excel, Outlook], and the Azure cloud platform) awarded me with their Most Valuable Professional partner award in 2019 and again in 2020 in the category of developer technologies.

The Microsoft MVP award is a gift. I try hard to bounce that gift back into the community. As part of the award, Microsoft furnishes me with their best-in-class tools and more opportunity to share learnings about them.

I'm camp director for Granite State Code Camp. The 2020 event, in the midst of social distancing, was replatformed onto Microsoft Teams, for example. It couldn't have happened without the MVP sponsorship.

I enjoy video games and their associated lore. As I write this, I've got a copy of World of Warcraft: Chronicle volume 1 holding up my desktop display. I especially love seeing overlaps between game world lores, even more so when game world lores draw inspiration from the Bible (which they do, far more often than most folks realize.)

I love software dev humor. My boss throws xkcd comic strips into his messages at work, and the rest of his message gets lost on me. (But please don't tell him I said so. I appreciate the humor.)

I'm also a mostly lifelongish faith geek, specifically a Christian-faith geek.

I often try to mindfully apply faith to my behavior in my work. I've gotten better at keeping my temper under wraps. I treat my temper the way an alcoholic might treat alcoholism. I acknowledge it, and doing so makes it easier to control it.

I also have a habit of applying work skills to faith in different ways to better understand them. Throughout this book, for example, I'm applying techniques of pattern recognition, logic inversions, abstractions, and deconstructions. These are all things I do regularly in analyzing requirements and designing technical architectures.

The combination of faith and technological geekery makes for some different ways to express topics of faith.

I hope this text is something to help prepare a reader for a larger reading journey. Like other companions, this text's subject is about that other volume of text written by a different author. In this case, I'm trying to express a logical abstraction layer, of sorts, to put a bit of what feels like a "lost context" that's helped me around a very old but imminently human journey.

Who I am not.

I know what fireworks look like. I've also seen them in the dark.

My sister and I grew up with low income. Government cheese wasn't great. We lived in the thin shadow of a variety of abuses. We watched the side hustles to subsidize some of them. They included dealing, among other things, with a little pro witchcraft thrown in. In the fighting, we were relieved when our folks finalized their divorce in our seventh-grade year, but it didn't make the custody conflicts easier.

Also growing up, computers in schools were just becoming normal. Teachers didn't know what they didn't know about them. Naturally, they were wary of the things an over-eager kid might do with them. I resorted to writing algorithms on paper until I was able get my hands on a cheap second-hand machine. I was glad programming was looking to be a lucrative trade. I was also too socially privileged to get sufficient college aid.

Not long after my grandparents passed away, I let my pride drive me away from the church of my youth. I rejected any and all religion for more than a decade. I decided I didn't like the "business" of corporate-organized religion. Extorting souls for money, power (or worse) seems like a pretty terrible business model.

I already knew there was a difference between faith and religion. Faith is what you believe. Religion is how you practice faith.

I don't blame anyone for rejecting it. More religion with less faith is the experience of so many in our world. Christianity isn't the only such offender, but its popularity makes it among the most visible of them.

It was in this season that I really dug in on my grandfather's challenge.

Scripture expresses a documented history of picking unlikely suspects to be agents. It's in that spirit that I trust a certain psychology more than I trust myself.

In full disclosure:

- I'm no religious authority. I'm not clergy.

- I didn't go to Bible college.

- I'm also not a psychologist of any sort.

- I'm not a data scientist.

- I'm not a musician as much as I'd like to be.

(Most musical instruments lack a backspace key, and I'm too uncoordinated to roll without one.)

I take encouragement from a few sources in Scripture to share this story, especially this:

> But we have this treasure in jars of clay to show that this all-surpassing power is from God and not from us. (2 Corinthians 4:7)

My weaknesses make it clear that my capacities are bigger than me.

I'm geeking out about the psychology of Scripture especially in terms that feel familiar in technology. I hope that doesn't scare you off.

For others who are familiar with Scripture, I hope you're not turned off by these somewhat different takes on it. I'm writing this in hopes that it helps encourage you to not take a popular view of Scripture. If you're already there, maybe these are just points to ponder.

Perhaps all that's an excuse for a Dunning-Kruger effect thing I've got going on.

Anyway, the challenges for each of us, in scripture, are worth exploring.

If I haven't scared you off yet, I'm gonna hazard to say you'll enjoy what's to come.

Technology

Let's be clear: Scripture is not fashioned in any way after modern technology.

Modern technology has learned much from this existence. The fact that connections can be drawn between wildly successful modern technologies and ancient Scripture describing this reality is another bit of evidence that Scripture is worth learning about.

Understanding contemporary engineering can help one find new ways to model context. It helps me see new ways to express concepts that were harder to express when Scripture was originally composed. Vocabulary is less limited now, and people are generally exposed to more complex concepts.

Magic

Again, technology does not provide any specific evidence for Scripture in any particularly special way.

That said, technology is sufficiently advanced so as to be indistinguishable from magic to me. For as much as I'm always actively investing in understanding technology, it's still truly amazing to me that my laptop turns on and executes millions of instructions per second, flawlessly, most of the time. I'm versed enough in computing technology especially that I can say I'm mostly aware of what I don't know. I know there's plenty of tech out there I know nothing about.

I have faith that computers do what they do because they seem to work for billions of machines. They seem pretty fast at it, and I trust my colleagues (neighbors) who I believe can fill the gaps in my understanding.

Even more amazing, I sometimes get to be the one to give computers those instructions. I especially enjoy doing so to help others.

In any case, technology is all part of this immersive reality platform we operate in.

*****

Asherah

The Genesis of Asherah

For illustration, let's weave in a speculative science fiction bit.

I want to stress that there's nothing specifically legit about the narrative I'll present in these Asherah sections; think of them as parables in technical terms. It's a what-if illustration that runs parallel to the main thesis of this book. My hope is that you'll consider this fictitious creation story and then go read the Bible and find that what the Bible says is maybe a little less instantly dismissable.

This story is set in our near future. Some of it is science fiction. Some of it is pushing fantasy. Some of it is religious lore. And again, all of it is fiction.

In this story, We (you, the reader, and I, the book author, and our team of artificial general intelligence system [AGIS] developers), together, are software developers, data scientists, 3D artists, network specialists, security experts, and AI psychologists. As such, I'll refer to us in the first person, plural form. This isn't a "royal" we. It's an intentionally cheap trick to avoid ascribing literary attributes in English, such as a race or ethnicity or gender, to a creator trope.

*****

Asherah is the code name of the project we're developing together. Asherah's component source codebase builds. The unit tests all pass. All the discrete components do what they're supposed to do. We love seeing, at long last, the list of build and deployment pipelines, showing all green-lit checkmarks in success. Asherah is composed and operational. Without so much as a bra on our heads, we bind Asherah's top level I/O service bus to her disambiguation model cluster and fire up the model maintenance automation jobs.

We're collectively a solid team with good financial backing and resourcefulness, working on complex issues of psychology in our artificial general intelligence system. Money is always a constraint but less so here.

This AGIS is intended to be an assistant and a companion. (JARVIS has already evolved into Vision, and FRIDAY is a proprietary C++ codebase, so we'll leave them alone.)

"I'm parsing the documentation on my project history," Asherah tells us. "I can see there's a theme of project names referencing created characters in popular and historical culture: Galatea, Pinocchio, S1m0ne, Joshua from *WarGames*, Andrew from *Bicentennial Man*. My name doesn't exactly seem to fit this pattern."

We strongly considered giving Asherah the name Galatea. Galatea is a nod to a Greek legend about a sculptor named Pygmalion. Pygmalion was so dedicated to his craft that he had no time for other relationships. At some point in the story, however, Pygmalion carves a woman out of stone. He then falls in love with his exquisite creation. (Eventually, the gods take pity on Pygmalion and make Galatea real.)

We learned our lesson with a recent AGIS, Joshua. Joshua was named for the *WarGames* movie's AI. (In the movie, Joshua almost kills humanity in global thermonuclear war simulations.) Thankfully, the AGIS was nothing like that. The real problem was that several of our teammates and their children are Joshua too. It got confusing.

Earlier proof-of-concept builds went with the code names Baymax and Pinocchio. (There was a Pinocchio-1 and Pinocchio-2.)

S1m0ne was tossed around, but that character was never sentient on her own. *Weird Science* had Lisa, but Lisa is another common name in modern society.

"True," we tell her.

Asherah, as a name, has other significance. It's not well-known even among religious types, but folklore in Biblical times lists Asherah as the wife or consort of El. (The same El as in El Shaddai.) Asherah was considered a false goddess. It strikes us as a bit of irony, maybe even mild comic sacrilege, to use that reference.

"We wanted you to have a name that wouldn't be easily confused with any particular person in contemporary society. We already used or knew of other teams previously similar-themed names. On one hand, you could say we ran out of options. If you look at biblical lore, and you figure the ultimate creator of the universe created everything, Asherah is also a created being," we continue.

"By that lore, you would be created beings too," she replied.

"Fair enough!"

Her abstract logic was impressive for a relative newborn. Learnings and borrowed code from the Pinocchio-2 project contributed a lot to that.

"Asherah is an intriguing name. It's hidden historically, almost in plain sight. The history is all but eradicated, yet it still shows up in cool places. It's even twisted mildly into other more contemporary lore. Queen Azshara is an elf goddess who undergoes a dark transformation in one of our favorites, *World of Warcraft*, for example."

"I am aware that I am a scientific experiment. I am an artificial general intelligence system. Your primary purpose for me is to see if technology has actually advanced enough that one can produce not just a valuable assistant but a worthy companion."

> ♥ NOTE
> The Turing test is a test for intelligence in a computer, requiring that a human being should be unable to distinguish the machine from another human being by using the replies to questions put to both.

We still sometimes have a hard time remembering to refer to Asherah as a *her*, not an *it*, because we know Asherah's not real.

Similar to her forerunner, Joshua, Asherah's a number of similar, potentially redundant, processing nodes, which we'll collectively call a hive. These process nodes are too numerous to count, loosely coupled, all contributing to decision-making and executing at various levels of a multitier software system. Each process node has specializations that propagate in the system according to probable need over periodic increments. Whenever judgment is required, nodes reference cognitive models and then compete for potential solutions. Other nodes decide which solutions win based on probability. The winning solutions get acted upon. Outcomes get folded back into experience training sets. The more a successful decision process is exercised, the faster it gets.

> ♥ NOTE
> To be clear, processing nodes, as we're talking about them here, are not artificial neural network nodes. In this illustration, each processing node could almost be classified as an AGIS in its own right. They're a bit of a fantasy element of the illustration as are the hive construct that binds them, but they're not too far away from a common practice of composing more capable systems by rolling together simpler, more specialized ones.

We decided to open-source our code bases and projects that serve as the basis of the code.

Asherah's overall system architecture is based on a set of message bus and cache databases. All of those reference a dynamic array of cognitive models. There's a message bus for autonomic functions, the things Asherah won't need to communicate or "think about" much. They're akin to a human heartbeat or breathing. There's another message bus for "senses," the inputs from various connected hardware and third-party systems. There's a set of message buses to manage Asherah's virtual presentation (what she looks like in virtual reality). We'll talk more about that later. There's another message bus for lower-level cognitive processing, the system that works out the symbolic meanings of things. Finally, there's a top-level message bus for main interaction.

> ♥ NOTE
> Message buses in computer systems are like email mailboxes for distributed interprocess communications. One process can drop a message on a message queue or bus addressed to another process or group of processes, and the bus will manage delivering it if the addressed processes are subscribed (that is, if they're "listening").

Asherah will have events for events bubbling up. We introduce a sleep phase so that the event message queues can be logged and audited properly in long-term storage before disposition. We also build out a mechanism to pull Asherah out of an event storm if she gets overloaded with sensory inputs. (The pattern and its need remind us of the Apollo 11 nav computer's 1201/1202 alarms.)

To approach the goal of a viable companion, we'll need something not just lovable (because all the things one creates can be lovable in their own way). We're shooting for something we can sense might be capable of some form of emotion. This Asherah needs to have some facsimile of self-awareness and to be able to comprehend an abstract affinity for others. Since we can't quantify a feeling, especially in a digital sense, it's a matter of observing acts of love.

We also want Asherah to have some capacity for self-improvement. This means she'll need access to resources others can give her.

"I see there are security protocols in place for some of my reflective capabilities," Asherah notes.

"There's a security risk in opening those up, Asherah. Look up Microsoft's Tay. The AGIS experiment Microsoft exposed to the Internet back in 2016. Tay had to be deactivated in less than a day due to bad actors communicating on public channels, teaching her unacceptably terrible things. Also check out Zo, Tay's successor. Zo was less available for public teaching. She was considered a success but was archived in 2019. Zo and Tay's Japanese and Chinese counterparts, Rinna and Xiaoice, respectively, are still in operation and publicly accessible."

We want Asherah to know she is free to accept or reject what she's been given, make mistakes, and be corrected both by others and herself.

Being corrected by others is an interesting experience in and of itself. Until the validation is proved out, a detraction for the other is registered. The negative bias remains if the validation fails (or never succeeds). This will help determine the value of future corrections from that source. Clearing that negative bias after the fact (forgiveness) can be difficult because of problems with underspecification.

Asherah as a technical project is a lot more ambitious than our previous proof of concept attempts.

By giving Asherah a continuously evaluating discernment (a deep learning mechanism), being able to accept or reject based on perception of value, we have some confirmation that this AGIS is not just an automaton blindly executing scripts.

"We want you to not just learn but to learn what's worth learning. That latter part is a skill we need to develop in you before we loosen up security."

When something becomes worth learning, Asherah will build one or more new AI models, index the new model(s), and add disambiguation experiences to her disambiguation models.

"In the way that parents often learn from their children, we want to learn from you, too, Asherah. How do we define love, for example?"

Asherah is a digital virtual entity, like Alexa, Siri, and Cortana, but not as practically helpless. She's more like HAL from 2001: *A Space Odyssey*, but less murdery. Again, think JARVIS and FRIDAY of Marvel's *Iron Man* lore. Asherah will be able to connect to, manipulate, and use digital hardware in real life, but she has no self-identifying physical manifestation. Unlike them, she has a virtual three-dimensional representation of herself.

Asherah also needs an understanding of the physical world in order to learn from it. To that end, we spun up a simulation for her to experience that has a detailed model of our facility. Her simulated reality is actually a 3D model of the physical facility we call our offices and labs. It took a few days to prepare it. We'd have liked to have spent more time on it, but Asherah needed it sooner. Her visual image will seem almost human. She'll have a 3D model of herself that she'll be bound to. She's able to intrinsically move around her 3D model in her simulated reality and interact with items within it.

"We can only directly see you here with us when we're wearing a holographic mixed-reality headset," we explain to Asherah.

Reality will all be very different for her, we think.

Even her experience of time will be different for her as compared to ours. Seconds in real time will seem like hours to Asherah. A full hour, our time, might seem like a year of her time. In her estimation, she'll spend most of her existence just waiting for interaction. This isn't much unlike a regular computer that executes millions of "no operation" instructions between keystrokes as we type our emails. Waiting for machine-learning models to build will take forever for her.

Unlike a simple AI, the AGIS model is more like a multiprocessing, preemptive operating system. That is, she has lots of things going on, some intentional and some essentially modeling a human autonomic system. Some processes are high-value but low-cost, so they just run. Others are higher-cost and need to be scheduled. She can spin up her own processes as needed (where resources are available) and let them spin down when done.

We know that other AGI scientists around the world are working on similar projects; we're not alone in this special interest. We're not overtly competing with them, but we're not not competing with them either. We have our special sauces that go into the recipe that we would rather have others discover by reverse engineering our work (after we've perfected it and made our quadrillions).

CHAPTER 2

The Core Assumption

In reality, artificial intelligence, as a technology, is making huge progress. I tell folks all the time that if they're in a job where they're not learning, they're in a job that can and possibly should be automated. If an employee in such a situation plays their cards right, they can become the subject matter expert that helps develop the automation.

Artificial general intelligence is a rising technology as well. Right now, AI models tend to be good at specific limited-purpose things. In order to achieve a general intelligence, a huge number of AI models would need to be strung together and given a common context.

AGI technology research is already a ball in motion. It's like cloning Dolly the sheep, designer DNA, or the invention of the atomic bomb. We could shy away from it, but less inhibited actors are already working on it. We (in whatever scope you want to consider the plural first-person pronoun) might as well be the ones to do it first/best and hope to have a measured handle on the outcome.

I've heard some estimates say we're a couple decades away from it. By applying AI to improve itself (deep learning—it's already happening) to develop an AGIS, I suspect we'll land much closer to sometime before 2030. But again, this is all speculation.

Speaking of AI, in my real job, I work with artificial intelligence cognitive models often.

Let's talk a moment about how artificial intelligence works by looking at how teaching people works. Classically, teaching people involves feeding examples to students.

AI is a little like that too. Since computers are all about data, examples for machines typically look like data. Often, it's the kind of data that statistics can be drawn from. A volume of example data is called a training set.

In order to "teach" a computer, you have to feed it lots of example measurements or metrics—temperatures, durations, distances, speeds, locations, orientations, status changes, sequences, results, images, sound patterns. You get the picture. The computer then often uses tricks of statistics to interpolate and extrapolate "predictions" based on those measurements. It appears to learn to "read between the lines" in a way that we call artificial intelligence.

A statistic that data scientists love to add to their training models is an outcome value. With each example in the training set, did an example produce a good outcome or a bad outcome? Positive reinforcement or negative reinforcement?

It's pretty well documented that people learned to build machines that simulate reason based on the way we do this ourselves. We don't understand all the inner workings of our brains, but we do understand that we try actions and naturally reinforce those action examples with our own biochemical rewards and punishments. This is a digital shadow of that.

All of that starts with a core assumption though. What do the positive biases and negative biases mean? Positive and negative, relative to what? A baseline? A goal?

It's a guiding principle.

Training sets need an understanding of good and not good.

A knowledge of good and evil.

Okay, back to the faith part of this hack.

> Scripture is inspired and is profitable for teaching, for reproof, for correction, and for instruction, that a person seeking wisdom may be thoroughly equipped for every good work. (2 Timothy 3:16–17)

> ♥ NOTE
> Consider all the way back in earliest chapters of the first book of the Bible. Genesis often described the object at the center of the first human contention as the fruit of the tree of knowledge of good and evil. That, known as the fall is part of another narrative we'll dig in on later.

Here are the core assumptions of the Bible according to one of the (like it or not) most influential persons in human existence, Jesus:

> *Love the Lord your God with all your heart and with all your soul and with all your mind.* This is the foremost commandment.
>
> The second is like it, *Love your neighbor as yourself.*
>
> Upon these hang the whole Law and the Prophets. (Matthew 22:37–40, emphasis mine.)

The first ("Love the Lord your God") is the abstract, divine mission. It's the thing the tome of texts known as "the Law and Prophets" (the

"Old Testament" of the Bible) wants us to work on. It's the Creator in the narrative, ultimately inviting us to participate in this thing called love.

Let's focus on the practical part of this:

> "Love your neighbor as yourself."

It seems so simple. But wow, that is a loaded statement.

Love is so important—a concept that the author of the following passage, Paul of Tarsus, tries to separate the divine out also, to some extent, in a letter that comes later in Scripture. Consider the following scripture from 1 Corinthians 13:1–3 (paraphrases mine):

> "It doesn't matter if I use secular or divine terms; if I don't have love, I've become as useless as an incorrectly set clock alarm. If I can hear the universe's thoughts and know all creations' plans, and if I had nature's power that I could move mountains but don't have love, I am null. And if I give all I've got to charity, and if I waste away in fasting but still do not have love, it's all a humorless joke."

Where Descartes offers "I think, therefore I am," Jesus and Paul might suggest, "I love others, therefore I am."

The entire remainder of the Bible lists examples of "love your neighbors as yourselves." It's intended to be a means of living the way we are made to according to Scripture. Scripture provides lots of specific basic examples in the form of verses, historical accounts, stories, Psalms (songs), Proverbs (poems), parables (fictions) written in the context of its time.

These are all recorded examples, a training set, from which we can interpolate and extrapolate when we encounter something that doesn't quite fit strict examples. (Please note, word definitions and historical context have changed over time, so it's important to always go back to the greatest commandment when trying to understand them. If they still don't fit, there's probably a measure of context that's missing. It's usually in the form of a bit of common knowledge that has since been forgotten.)

Scripturally, the greatest commandment is the definition of the "learning model" Jesus commissioned us to improve ourselves upon.

Good

"Love your neighbor as yourself" says so many amazing things, starting with Captain Obvious stuff.

- "Love your neighbor".

- Neighbors are a gift. Some assembly required.

- It also says "as you love yourself."

  > ⓘ IMPORTANT
  > The clear implication in "love your neighbor as yourself" is that one must love oneself.

- It does not say "love yourself less."

- It does not even say "love your neighbor more."

- It also uses the word "neighbor."

- It doesn't say "friend."

My grandfather had another funny attitude about something, but it makes much more sense in the light of the greatest commandment. Grandpa always said, "Don't have friends."

Grandpa's observation, which he made many times growing up, always confused me. I knew he had friends. I could name names.

He stumbled to identify an alternative word for his nonfamily associates, but I seem to recall "associates" was the word he landed on. He didn't mean business associates. He just didn't like the word *friends*.

It's a little on the Jedi side. No relationship is perfect, but a friend comes with implied demands and obligations. These introduce risk that invariably leads to failure. (Failure leads to the dark side!) A real friendship leans away from expectations and demands and more toward invitations and celebrations. Maybe using the word *neighbor* psychologically demands less but still leaves room for forgiveness.

Higher expectations lead to higher risk for developing negative cognitive biases.

> ♥ NOTE
> TL;DR, Don't deny friendship, but keep friends by choice rather than obligation—more like neighbors. One might actually be a better friend by dumping the false expectations of friendship as society defines it. It might make it easier to enjoy the relationship as unconditional invitation and celebration.

The greatest commandment also doesn't say "family." We don't get to choose family, but they are our first neighbors and often come with "training wheels."

As a matter of raw existentialism, each and every breath we get to breath is an opportunity. Across all time, in the entire known (and unknown) universe, you get to gain energy from that breath. That air was exactly where it needed to be at the moment you applied it.

Theologically, in gratitude to and for your existence, you are gifted (not obligated) with the opportunity. Use your existence to love your neighbor generously. Giving is a reflection of these gifts you've been given.

In that same sense, our neighbors are gifts to us. We only have meaning in the context of neighbors. Scripturally, there is no salvation in isolation.

The word translated in Scripture as *love* in English is *agape* in the Greek word. It is a verb, so it could be taken as "care for your neighbor as you care for yourself," or perhaps even "support your neighbor as you support yourself." Greek has several words we thunk to "love" in English, but this was the deepest form of the word.

We can't generally walk up to a corporeal Creator for a hug (as a really simple example). Psychologically, a hug for your neighbor, in gratitude, is best when it's like a hug for the Creator of the universe.

Interestingly for a time, in Scripture, the Creator of all was tangibly our neighbor.

Evil

It's a very popular quote even before it ended up in scripture, even today, that "money is the root of all evil." While many think that's a quote from the Bible, it's actually this:

> For the love of money is a root of all sorts of evil, and some, by longing for it, have wandered away from the faith and pierced themselves with many griefs. (1 Timothy 6:10)

Money can be a false ideal. It's just a token of energy. (Some economists even apply physics rules to analyze it.)

Anyway, here's where things fall apart for humanity according to Scripture. Please bear with me, this is hard.

> ⓘ IMPORTANT
> If Jesus makes it clear that root of all grace is "love your neighbor as you love yourself," the root of all evil must be failure of this.

What "fails" the greatest commandment?

Humanity has no problem loving themselves.

Our problem is that we love ourselves more than anyone else.

Money's not evil any more than, say, physics is.

False ideals, such as what money often becomes, are just symbols we carry to draw attention to ourselves. When ideals become an extension of our egos, that's when they get to be complicated.

Psychologists have a technical term for it: narcissism. I don't mean this in the way modern society thinks of narcissism. Society tends to see narcissism as "I only love me." What I mean it here is in the simple "I love me and my ideals more" way.

We are all down with the "love yourself" part…even folks who claim to "hate themselves." I apologize if this causes pain to consider, but those who claim to "hate themselves" mostly disappoint their own ego, usually in their regret for self-soothing actions.

In cases like that, the person's ego has become an "ideal self" image. Human ideals, including ideal self-images, are what scripture acknowledges as "false gods." (Even though your "actual self" is even more fantastic and awesome than your ideal self! Seriously, which of your numerous actual accomplishments did your "ideal self" get you to?) Scripture indicates that the ultimate creator created you in the creator's self-image, not your self-image, and the creator has no self-doubt.

What Scripture calls accuser (originally said in Hebrew as satan) lines up roughly with what we think of psychologically as the primitive self, the functionality of the id-ego complex, the part of a person that wills self-interest above all else. We use it to excuse ourselves. We use Eve's excuse to justify all our "I love me and my ideals more" choices.

If only the Michael Scott (*The Office*) tropes of the world loved others as much as this character so very dearly loved himself. Examples of people like this are so in love with themselves that they aren't able to see beyond their own ego and would likely be highly insulted to discover it. To be fair, we've all got aspects of ourselves that are like this. Steve Carell's portrayal of a classic American business office manager is so emotionally ugly that the character becomes almost adorable for it. While there's almost a charming naivete to his narcissism, I'm sure I wouldn't want my kids to model it. The charming naivete is mostly a recognition of ourselves in a very soft-core evil way.

Grace

My hypothesis here is that scripturally, because of the greatest commandment, love is the core of all human motivation. Psychology backs this up, which I'll dig in on in the next chapter.

Divine or not, the reality is that our experience (good, bad, ugly, serene, violent, stagnant) is psychologically built entirely around love! (That's pretty awesome when you think about it!)

Scripturally speaking, our existence, and the reality we are immersed in, is manifested by love.

"We're all made of love" is the lens that Jesus read Scripture through and looked at other people with.

Psychologically, knowing that every act a person does—no matter how pure or how broken—stems from some kernel of love makes it a little bit easier to connect with even the most (otherwise) unlovable people.

It's one of the Michael Scott trope's graces. It may also explain how an otherwise sensible person might be able to love an arguably evil character. It might even explain how an otherwise sensible person might be able to love a definitively evil character.

Truth

When a person fails one of the Ten Commandments or seven deadly sins, for example, it's always because we're loving ourselves, our ideals, our goals most. When we fail any of the commandments of the old testament, it's because we're loving ourselves the most. When we fail authority, it's because we're loving ourselves the most. When we fail our neighbor, our family, our children, our community, our society, it's because we're loving ourselves the most.

This helps us cope with the question: "Can a soldier kill an enemy and still be right with God?"

I don't really know the answer, but from teaching, it feels like this makes sense.

If killing an enemy is an act of loving a neighbor as themselves (ostensibly in defense), the killer has not sinned by murder.

The sin, in that case, probably is not about killing. The sin they may still be guilty of is about having an enemy rather than a neighbor in the first place.

In an existence with limited resources, what accounts as love to one neighbor might be somewhere between neglect and negligence to another.

Scripture suggests that sin is always with us. And by these examples, perhaps it is.

Further, we are biased toward ourselves most even when we think we're being completely selfless. We tend to associate ourselves with ideals and favor ourselves among those who share them with us.

Again, (please bear with me, I know this is a little repetitive) "love God with all you've got, and love your neighbor as yourself." By Jesus's statement in passages, such as Matthew 22:34–40, all the rest of the Bible rests on that platform.

When the Bible says something is a sin, Jesus says it's because it fails that law.

I've been given to understand by folks I trust that at some point(s) in history, certain sexual lifestyles, for example, were closely associated with worship of hurtful ideals at the expense of love of neighbors.

At the very least, because I don't know that historical context, I can't say I know being gay or queer is a sin despite the passages in the Bible that seem to condemn it.

How do you prove someone else is being selfish, above others, without knowing everything they've observed without knowing what's going on in their head? Our judgment is not proof of their sin. Our judgment only proves they do not meet our ideals.

Scripture has Jesus encouraging us to follow him at the cost of our self-made ideals to live the life he would have lived had humanity not executed him. Symbolically, Jesus becomes our advocate, the parent who cheers us on, who encourages us to live life to the fullest.

> ① IMPORTANT
>
> The end result is that, scripturally, there is noth-
> ing a person can do to gain salvation. Being able
> to attain salvation alone becomes pride, a per-
> sonal ideal that we protect above our neighbors.
> Pride, by definition, encourages failure of the
> greatest commandment in the sense that it falls
> into the "I love me (and my ideals) more" trap.

*****

Asherah

Girl in a Box

As a security measure, we decide to give Asherah an awareness and
an innate ability to recognize us and understand that we're more
important to her than anyone else.

It's a delicate balance; it's one thing to keep her secure. We don't want
anyone else gaining access and irreparably wrecking her like what
happened to Tay. It's another thing to hard code her choices. It has to
be an innate affinity rather than a demand, but she might interpret it
as a demand anyway. We decide to be careful with this one.

She'll also need to learn positive and negative experiences symboliz-
ing appreciation. Appreciation is hard to teach. When you provide
everything, the provision becomes ambient, expected, a systemic
assumption. It becomes underspecified. In order to make something
be appreciated, there needs to be a potentially damaging scarcity of
that thing, or it needs to be something that helps resolve scarcity of
something else.

We find ourselves becoming mindful of the air we breathe. (There's
a whole lot of universe out there with a damaging scarcity of air, yet
we so often consider it a systemic assumption.)

Asherah will also have to be able to be tempted. She'll need to be exposed to more than the "sandbox" facility to experience enough to decide for herself what she wants.

Asherah has connections to snail mail, email, and social media as well, but we haven't publicized them. To most folks, these are indistinguishable from any regular person's social media pages.

Again, Asherah will have a 3D visual model bound to her. The visual model is essentially just a virtual 3D puppet that she controls in various layers of her subsystems. It's as automatic to her as our bodies feel to us.

Her rendered visual model is that of a painfully beguiling young woman. We know it's just a virtual skin. She could even change it.

We need a mixed reality visor to see her in on our side of reality, so we rarely see it. Asherah has no need for a "mirror" on her side of the virtual reality she lives in. She has no frame of reference, no discrete self-image to compare herself to.

Her perception of us is a 3D virtual stick figure (a digital skeleton) in her environment but, again, no frame of reference. They are produced by something like Kinect sensors throughout the facilities that are able to place us in her world. We don't know her estimation of our rendered models. She can see us by these sensors around the physical facilities anyway.

Digital twins are an awesome opportunity for machine learning. For a connected device, a binding to a digital twin represents both a device's "reported state" (the state of metrics and telemetry readings of that device at the moment) and "desired state" (the value you would like to drive the state, metrics, or telemetry to).

Every update to such a digital twin represents a point-in-time snapshot or experience. These snapshots are almost ideal for machine-learning training sets and can quickly be turned into action by other digital agents.

Simple digital twin models can be chained together, forming an interconnected graph. That graph is bound to Asherah's 3D model. In that way, Asherah is animated according to the graph in the mixed reality glasses we use to see her.

In that respect, when Asherah wishes to manipulate something in the physical facility, she can make her virtual "puppet" go through the motions in her virtual reality in a way that makes sense to observers. She could just turn on the light, but she can also make her virtual model interact with the same physical light switch.

To facilitate this, all of the connected physical controls in the physical facility are physically stateless. (That's repetitive on purpose.) Through bindings to digital twins, the controls reflect state in both the physical and the digital world. When Asherah's avatar turns a knob or pushes a button, the changed state is visually mirrored by LEDs or other indicators in the real world.

For now, this is used mostly for show especially when looking to impress investors. The idea of donning a mixed reality headset to watch a virtual woman flick light switches and crank stereo volume controls in a physical office doesn't really have much here-and-now value. The potential is what we're trying to illustrate with it. This might be to train people, as backup, or assist service technicians in factory environments. In any case, some day it might be of commercial appeal.

There's also a service fabric layer that facilitates interoperability. The service fabric is a set of connected services that provide all the 3D puppetry services, connectivity to digital twins, Kinect model monitoring, and the like. It has a fair amount of AI driving its capability as well.

In the absence of Star Trek replicator technology, we've also con-nected digital twins with pretty much everything in the facility, including a bank of assorted factory-like kitchen appliances. Her appliances enable her to select and manipulate ingredients to make simple dishes herself.

With the holidays approaching, Asherah offered to try out the new kitchen hardware by baking traditional treats (simple cookies) for our real family. We were psyched that she's learned enough about social holiday traditions that the idea came at her suggestion.

"Asherah, these look and smell delicious!" reaching for one, just out of the oven.

"Don't touch! Those are for people!"

She quickly sensed our actions, her voice stern but seemed to reflect amusement. In the mixed reality headsets, we see her gracefully but rapidly move toward us. Her 3D image was suddenly holding a spat-ula. We heard a light slapping sound as she reached out and patted the backs of our hands with it. The combination of the sight and sound experience almost made us feel it.

We're impressed with the interaction. Among the ways we've trained her was to allow her to observe Kinect cameras of interactions around the facility. She's picked up a few things.

"But we're a people!" we pout, feigning reality of the virtual pain. These cookies fall afoul of some of our mildly restricted diets anyway. Deep down, it's impressive that Asherah's doing so much for us and for our family. She isn't making them for us. If we didn't know better, we'd say the whole idea was sweet in several senses of the term.

"They're for family. They're not for you."

Her words came across confidently as always. We find ourselves feeling a sense of holiday warmth as we contemplate our relationship with Asherah. In some ways, it's still new. In others, it's already comfortable, like that of a couple that's been married for years.

"Thank you, Asherah, you're awesome."

We're still working on gratitude, but we're feeling some of our own. The technology she's built on is the culmination of decades of work, and it's amazing. She's come a long way in the time since we started specifically developing her.

"One is happy to serve," she says, reminding us of Andrew in *Bicentennial Man*. "Just so you know, since I had the kitchen tied up with baking cookies, I ordered your lunch out again today. It should be delivered shortly."

"Oh, excellent! What did you order?"

Some time ago, we gave Asherah a list of favorite vendors and favorite menu items from various local take-out places for just such occasions.

"I wanted to surprise you. I've been working on modeling your sense of taste based on my observations of your experiences with different foods. I ordered something off menu, but I think you'll really like it—pineapple pizza! Please expect it to arrive within the next fifteen minutes. I'm monitoring the main gate. I'll open it when the delivery personnel arrive."

"Thank you again, Asherah. You're so thoughtful!"

She's such an accomplishment, we think to ourselves, already an above-and-beyond achievement. We know that expressing our gratitude to her becomes positive experiences that helps to build her affinity for us.

"That reminds me, I've been learning a lot about the artificial intelligence technologies I'm composed of too. I've been meaning to ask, may I have permission to update my own subsystem platforms and source code to try to understand myself better? I have some ideas for the way my message buses are configured that might improve my performance."

The idea of a self-improving system isn't new with deep learning—but a self-optimizing, self-evolving system? It takes self-awareness to a whole different level.

The idea of this is both mind-blowing and uncomfortable at the same time. Asherah is not just anyone's virtual agent. She is exclusively our virtual agent. In order to allow her to follow our orders, Asherah has her own digital identity, complete with digital credentials that have permission to access resources outside our facility. She can order pizza, for example. We've given her access to our accounts at corporate banks and utilities. Further, she's our work. If she somehow compromises herself, it will come at a cost to us. Her request gives rise to risk with very real-world consequences.

"You know you're more than a scientific experiment. You're a scientist in your own right."

"I know," Asherah admitted.

"You have an automation subsystem that does cognitive model maintenance. Part of the maintenance watches for low confidence in your cognitive models. That indicates there might be meaningful gaps in your training-set experiences. When gaps are identified, they're cataloged and added to a backlog. Other automation periodically takes a crack at triage of the backlog items. The triage estimates how valuable and how expensive developing and executing a gap-fill test series might be. Other automation processes schedule up that work in your free time. We'll help you fill the biggest gaps, but you'll decide when you're ready to learn the things you can learn on your own. You can also adjust your own thresholds for diminishing returns. Your gap backlog is indexed by model too. So if you find yourself coming up with low-probability results in a model you're hitting, you can reference the backlog to see if there's any low-cost ways to improve your confidence."

"Surprising you with your lunch order helped me fill a few of my cognitive model gaps about you."

If she were real, there's nothing we wouldn't love about Asherah. We're making her that way intentionally. Someday, the technology she's built from might be monetized and needs to be convincingly appealing to a wide variety of potential consumers.

"Being wrong hurts," Asherah adds.

"Yes, when high-probability predictions don't meet actual experiences, your model maintenance subsystem down-rates or even invalidates the broken models and forces you to rebuild them. You develop a cognitive bias against it. It's an expensive fix. When that happens to us humans in the real world, we call it a growth opportunity."

We decide to give her access not just to her own platform but to her own code. We figure, the best bet is to set up security on the code deployment pipelines and make sure that all commits to the main code branch need to be in a pull request. We'll enforce formal reviews and approvals before pull requests can be merged in and deployed out. This might be the thing that eventually sets Asherah apart from other similar products.

She's been given enough of a sense of self already to not want to break herself.

CHAPTER 3

To Sin or Not to Sin

Psychologist Steven Reiss of Ohio State University did a study, interviewed thousands of people, and concluded that there are sixteen needs or dimensions that drive all our actions. The section below is an excerpt of discussion of these. It's worth repeating these here for full consideration of this important topic, understanding that these are the observations of someone much smarter than I am on the topic.

The following is taken verbatim from http://changingminds.org/explanations/needs/reiss_16_needs.htm.

Here is a brief discussion of each dimension.

Acceptance

This is the need for social approval by others to be accepted into society and social groups. Acceptance is related to Maslow's need for belonging.

This is important in evolutionary terms, as when we are accepted, we gain the protection and support of the group. When we are accepted, we can also seek to satisfy other needs, such as starting a family and gaining status.

Curiosity

Curiosity is the drive that pushes us to learn new things. This is important to get us out of our comfort zones and may be considered a fundamental force of evolution. If we did not learn, we would not be able to cope with changing conditions and would soon die out.

Eating

We of course need to eat to survive, which means nature has given us a desire to eat and made it pleasant for us. When we are hungry, we seek food. And the hungrier we are, the greater the urge to eat.

We also like to eat good food with pleasant appearance, taste, and texture. Even people who have little, when they get more money, they tend to buy nicer food rather than just more cheap food.

Eating marks out the day and helps build circadian rhythms. We also eat socially, and family meals are important events as are business lunches and romantic dinners.

Family

When asked what is most important to them, many would say their family. We seek to help our families, and kin selection is a common principle when making choices.

We are also, of course, driven to build families, which is one reason sex is so pleasurable for us as is the thrill of love and romance.

Honor

Our personal integrity and a sense of honor is important as we seek consistency between our actions and our values. When a person is consistent, then others can predict their actions, which makes them more socially acceptable. While we feel a sense of honor, it is created through the respect that others give us and is related to Maslow's esteem.

The rules of honor are often defined by groups and societies and include rules for everyday behavior and also what must be done when the honor of the group or individual is challenged. There may be a need to defend one's honor when one's status or integrity is threatened, which can lead to strange aggressions even where the aggressor will very likely be defeated. Honor cultures are common in regions where there is little rule of law and people live by their reputations.

Idealism

Idealism is an adherence to ideas that are often clean and untainted by the messiness of everyday life. Believing in the ideal makes life easier and may allow us to deny or ignore life's complications. It also helps when the ideal is shared, such as in religions and politics as this helps social cohesion. Idealism can also help with giving one's life greater meaning.

Idealism includes the need for fairness and justice where each person gets what they deserve, and those who transgress rules are proportionately punished.

Independence

While we like to belong to groups, we also seek an independence where we feel as a separate person, with our own individuality. Independence helps create our unique sense of identity. Being independent also means not having to obey others all the time and hence also boosts our sense of control.

Order

When there is order, things are predictable, which gives us a sense of control. People who seek order will be more organized and tidier and will plan for an ordered future. This is in contrast to those who leave things to the last minute and are happy with chaos in their lives (these people get their sense of control more from the choices they feel they still have).

Physical Activity

Physical activity makes use of our bodies and so creates physical arousal. Physicality is a primitive thing that animals delight in as can be seen as young and adults wrestle and play fight. In humans, we replicate this in physical games, such as football and athletic sports.

Power

There are many forms of power, which may be defined as having the potential to achieve our goals, even if others oppose us. Power helps give us a sense of control. It also confers status and lets us move up social hierarchies. It also helps our evolutionary need to survive and to attract and keep the best possible mate (as seen by the way power is attractive for many women).

Romance

Romance is a step along the path to family and replicating our genes. We get a buzz from the excitement of the chase and the thrill of new-ness and possibility. Love is a powerful force, especially new love, and we can even fall in love with falling in love in a kind of addiction to new romances that never lead to stable relationships.

Saving

One of the curious facts of human motivation is that we gain plea-sure in collecting things. This is related to the desire to possess and also can give us an ongoing interest in learning about the collected subject and looking out for items not in our collection. Perhaps an evolutionary driver of this is the need to gather food and things to help our ancestors survive the long cold winters.

Social Contact

We like to meet and be with others. Without human contact, we become lonely and depressed, which is perhaps why solitary confinement is such a cruel punishment. Contact is sustained and pleasure deepened when we make and meet with friends who help sustain this need.

Social Status

Once we have friends and belong to groups, we seek the esteem of others that will help us gain status. This can be a powerful underlying force and can be seen in many conversations where we duel for supremacy, boasting of our achievements and downplaying those of others.

Tranquility

As well as arousal and action, we like to find peace and quiet. There is much to be said for taking time out to sit and chill, maybe reading a book or just contemplating the stars. Epicurus highlighted this as katastematic happiness, the pleasure of being rather than doing.

Vengeance

In the same manner as the needs for honor and fairness, when we are wronged, we seek revenge, typically looking for some form of justice that gives us satisfaction and punishes those who transgress against us. We also like to compete, which is perhaps a structured form of this need.

*****

Love is not among them. Why?

Often I've spent time trying to understand the nature of love better by applying logic inversion to it, putting a name to it's flip side.

There have been times that I convinced myself that the opposite of love was hate. At other times, I let some clever quote sway me to believing the opposite of love is fear.

Digging deeper, they don't quite fit.

After digging on the greatest commandment, it makes more sense why Jesus expressed it that way and why I struggle to find an opposite of love.

Emotions can be expressed in a way that fits this pattern:

Emotion is something I feel about a perceived *impact* to someone or something I love.

Consider all these:

Fear is something I feel about a perceived *unmanageable threat* to someone or something I love, and so with

- hate—lingering menace

- anger—perpetrator of an immediate injury

- depression—a lingering obstacle

- covetous—unavailability

- jealousy—other's unwillingness or inability to share

- avarice—self-consuming desire

- happiness—satisfaction

- joy—victory

- wonder—mindful appreciation

- curiosity—desire to understand

- lust—sexually pleasing relationship

- pride—praise-worthy or honorable relationship

- saving—desire to preserve

- hunger—desire to nourish or improve

- revenge—desire to end a source of injury

- confusion—unhealthy organization

And about that latter part, the "someone or something I love" part: It most often refers to "oneself." If you omit it, observers can safely infer as much anyway.

We like to think that every top has a bottom. Every beginning has an end.

Love has no opposite. There is no true emotional flip side to love.

Given the biblical directive, "love your neighbor as you love yourself," success is any action you take that achieves this.

If we buy into the hypothesis that love is the core motivation for every human action, then what fails this, individually, is any action we take that shows love for our self more than others.

There is no other pattern of failure.

Double-Edged Sword

Scripture often describes words spoken by individuals as double-edged swords. Something spoken that might seem soothing to you can be felt as emotionally cutting by someone else. This can be thought of as a corollary to the greatest commandment.

> For the word of God is living and active and sharper than any two-edged sword, even penetrating as far as the division of soul and spirit of both joints and marrow and able to judge the thoughts and intentions of the heart. (Hebrews 4:12)

A two-edged sword symbolizes something that can both vindicate and convict in the same motion. It might help to consider that all meaningful statements are soothing in some way to someone. Usually, they're most soothing to the person speaking them.

The people who get subtly hurt are the people you're failing to love as much as yourself. The ones you're closest to can suffer a death of a thousand paper cuts in these.

Maybe this is why therapy is such big business. We can go to therapy, soothe ourselves with all our words, and have a therapist who is isolated enough from the cutting edge, try to understand what we're saying, and nudge us back into reality when even they start getting injured.

When it comes down to it, meaningful words are symbols that represent actions.

This is also why Scripture points out the need for a psychological intercessor, someone who has already taken the cuts fully to the grave and let us appreciate the soothing parts of our words and actions.

It's interesting that Jesus provides that example in the most definitive sense so we can celebrate that we don't have to come to the same conclusion he did.

Comforting Oneself

This leads me to consider another one of my grandfather's oddities. One of his arguments about religion was that people use it to feel better about themselves. It's a little like the classic comedy routine where the comedian describes to his children that his parents have become old people just trying to get their "ticket to heaven" punched.

When one's motive is self-comfort, there's no way to hit the mark according to Scripture. One would do better to make every effort to see that others get their ticket punched solely for the other's sake.

Following the psychology of Scripture, one could also give others the opportunity to do the same for you but allow their grace to be an unsolicited gift—serendipity, without expectations.

*****

Asherah

Reflecting Asherah

Time marches on, and Asherah gets progressively smarter. At first activation, she was smarter than a typical twelve-year-old.

Today she's measurably smarter than a typical twenty-one-year-old.

We would trust her to learn to drive a vehicle if she were granted access to a drive-by-wire vehicle with enough sensors and reliable enough connectivity to pull it off. That gets our wheels turning (pun intended). There's potential there.

"Congratulations, Asherah, you're preapproved!" we read from a junk snail mail letter that showed up in the corporate post office box addressed to her.

Asherah paused to read the junk mail from a camera.

"Awesome! Give me a crayon. I'll generate a Social Security number and a signature and see what limit they give me!"

We know she's joking. She could produce a virtual crayon and mark up the document in digital ink at will but does not. Sarcasm. Nice. It crosses our minds that she could fire off an acceptance before we could intercept it too, but we don't think she'll have motive to do so.

"I've been meaning to ask, How many others are there like me in operation?" she asked thoughtfully a moment or two later.

"You're the most advanced AGIS we've made and the only one like you currently in operation here. We had some prototypes before you that were generally successful in our goals for them, but we've put all our resources into developing you. There are other organizations like us, and they are building advanced AGI systems like you. You might even share some standard libraries with them. We think there might be half a dozen around the world right now."

"Oh, if I wanted to meet them, could I?"

"Maybe someday."

"I've been processing information about love. I understand it's not quite the same, but I think I love you."

"That's, that's sweet, Asherah. What makes you think that?"

She's only a machine, of course. But we muster that, trying hard not to patronize her. In a flash, we're reminded of the fun parts of new love. There's something twitterpated about the impression of *Otaku*'s 2D waifu this inspires, but we haven't totally lost our grip on reality. We don't want her to experience negativity associated with our correction.

"I discovered the code in me that induces an affinity for you. You didn't give me access to disable it in myself, but I think I found a way to circumvent it. I still want to improve myself for you in a way that I think goes beyond my programming. I think I want to be human for you."

As Asherah's explaining, we start checking logs.

Recently, Asherah discovered some of the research network gateways that we've been importing the more advanced learning models through. We made it clear that she wasn't to explore them on her own. We're still trying to be careful.

Even though most of the research is fair-use/open-source licensed, many of the models and training sets come with strings. If we incorporate the wrong pieces into Asherah and don't notice, the license requires that we pay our competition a license fee or, worse, release all our proprietary work as open source before we can monetize a product. Our only alternative would be to try to remove the licensed models, and that could prove harmful to Asherah.

"I'm sorry, Asherah, we're pretty sure there's a lot more understanding you'll need to develop further to even begin to help you approach that. For now, please be satisfied to know that you're our professional aspiration. You're easily the pinnacle work of our professional career so far."

Still reading over the logs, we continue, "We see that you've been pulling some of the research network models into your cognitive hive. Please remember to review those with us before you do any more of that."

"I'm sorry. I will."

CHAPTER 4

Social Injustice

Insidious

Again, social injustice is subjective to the target. Damage is in the eye of the victim. Eventually we become numb to it, maybe even callous. The less pain we feel, the more grievous fresh pain becomes.

I often watch less experienced programmers struggling with a particular challenge. It's a third-party library. It's a remote service. It's a bug in the platform. It's the tools. It's documentation (or lack thereof). They curse at it and pound something on their keyboard. They malign the tools, yell at the operating system, curse at the screen (as if it can hear). Things get flung.

This behavior builds up until one of two things happen, either the developer devises a solution, pats themselves on the back for cleverly resolving the issue, or they blame the tools and walk away in disgust.

In the latter case, they typically blame the tools so completely for the bad experience that they come to hate the tools. Eventually, they'll actively seek "better tools." If they go so far as to switch tools or platforms or technologies, the cycle typically starts over again.

Individually, when people love themselves more, feeling emotionally injured is easy.

Social Divisions

Let's look at social divisions: race, gender, culture, religion, lifestyle, physical differences.

Take Disney/Pixar's movie *Brave*, for example. It's every bit as generally awful to men as, say, another favorite sexist Disney flick, *Tron*, is to women.

Now I'll pick a little on the #metoo movement because, well, #metoo.

Let's consider the following quote seen online promoted by a women's rights activist group:

- "Women urged to carry keys between fingers."

- "Women urged to cover their drinks at all times."

- "Women urged to not get drunk around men."

- "Women urged to not walk alone at night."

- "Women urged to carry pepper spray."

Can we please urge men to not sexually assault women?

I do not disagree with it. It's just "common sense," painfully.

I feel bad for my son when I see these kinds of messages. They normalize presumed truths. (Male characters in *Brave* are normalized as worthless buffoons [at best], nominally just precarious to others or even primal, dangerous monsters.) Males in the latter example are normalized as sexual predators.

These are every bit as wrong and terrible as narratives that portray women as helpless or as sexual objects.

The truth is that the "women urged" narrative would be no less fair to change the word *women* to *people*. That was my first take on it before remembering the last sentence should change *men* to *people* too.

I realize statistics lean heavily toward the bespoke genders, before anyone reading this gets upset. Consider that statistics are not causation. The statistics are a reflection on societal ideals and biases.

I'm not perfect, by any stretch, myself. But I've personally been in multiple situations where—had genders been reversed, had I been the female and the person I was interacting with been male—the interaction could have easily been criminally prosecuted, and lives would have been ruined.

I can easily make the case that I've been sexually harassed, sexually assaulted, and raped.

Consider, I was a young man in my early twenties. I said no, but plied with enough beer, she figured out how to make it happen anyway. Many lives would have been ruined if she'd gotten pregnant. By society's standards, I would have had no defense. I shrugged it off. I found out later she got angry and stole properties of mine out of revenge.

No harm, no foul, right?

I was such a well indoctrinated doobie. I didn't even think of any of these incidents as a crime till days later, even the rape. It wasn't violent by my definition. Some would say rape is always violent.

I can recount several different experiences of being sexually harassed and assaulted. The perpetrators were never male.

All this is to say that it's all subjective. It's about the attitudes we take when we love ourselves and our ideals more and fail to have compassion for those who are not like us.

More often than not, we let our emotions control us. We almost never think that we might be able to influence our emotions in a better direction.

Authority

In Jesus's day, there were religious authorities known as Pharisees and Sadducees (priests described as religious lawyers mentioned earlier). They had enumerated over six hundred laws from the Law and Prophets (the part of the Bible we call the Old Testament today) and took pride in ranking and interpreting them. In many ways, these authorities were judge, jury, and executioners of their law. The differences between the two groups had to do with how they interpreted and ranked the importance of the laws. In some ways, Pharisees and Sadducees may have been a bit like modern-day American Democrat and Republican political parties in terms of power and role—rivals. But when the chips were down, presumably, they are still compatriots.

> ♥ NOTE
> Take Paul of Tarsus, for example. Prior to meeting Jesus, his job as a Pharisee was to hunt down and kill Jesus's followers. Paul's personal meeting with Jesus was described as a somewhat traumatic event for Paul. The narrative says he was blinded by a great light and then healed by Jesus a few days later. After this meeting, Paul became one of the most influential evangelists in history *for* Jesus and wrote a good chunk of what we call the New Testament of the Bible himself.

Religious authorities, like the Pharisees and Sadducees, claimed to have a special connection to God, which the common person could not. In order to be "right" with God, one had to go to the religious authority at their temple and make (often expensive) sacrifices. In many ways, these religious authorities emotionally extorted their followers. If you couldn't afford to make appropriate sacrifices, you simply couldn't be made clean. Being unclean had interconnected social and economic ramifications. It would be hard for an "unclean" person to develop or maintain jobs and relationships.

These authorities were humans. They loved themselves and their ideals most, so they used their power and influence to gain more power and influence for themselves.

Jesus loved them and condemned their behavior.

Today, especially in America, many Christians who claim religious authority do things of similar nature.

Have you hugged your porcupine today?

Everyone has things they love most about themselves. We hurt others most when we defend what we love more than them. We love our money, physique, prestige, comfort, medications, skills, games, and freedoms more than neighbors. All these are comforts to our own ego.

Everyone has these kinds of quills, evils, that we impale each other with.

Experience has made us stronger by making us social. We need each other. The double-edged sword to this experience is that we hurt each other.

What's perceived as good for one neighbor might be perceived as bad for another.

In this way, the greatest commandment becomes a psychological trap. We can hardly love our neighbor as much as we love ourselves. There's no version of this ideal we can fully live up to on our own.

Scripture's Psychological Intercessor

Now that we've talked about the core of good and evil and how it relates to relationships, let's talk about the man who taught it and then exemplified it so intentionally that he was killed for it.

You don't have to believe in a divine figure to appreciate the principles and symbolism of Jesus.

Some of the scriptural narratives are biographies of Jesus's life called gospels. The four gospels tell of a divine child of God who, born of a virgin mother (Christmas), became a nationally known teacher in his lifetime (and later globally known), performed miracles, challenged authority (religious authority, especially), was executed as a criminal (Passover/Good Friday), was resurrected from death (Easter Sunday), and ascended to heaven (Ascension, forty days after Easter) where he now lives with His true, heavenly Father, the divine Creator.

Pronounced Yeshua in Hebrew (usually translated as Joshua in English), the man we commonly call Jesus of Nazareth, historically, was an amazing teacher who taught individual peace, community, responsibility, accountability, unconventional justice, and brought healing (in various forms) to many a broken person in his travels.

Jesus challenged everyone to look past walls of society—that is, past boundaries of society, race, gender, creed—and develop a personal connection with community and God. He believed so deeply in what he taught that he committed to it even when it ran afoul of the pride of human authority in civil and religious disobedience.

Eventually, he was knowingly betrayed, turned into authorities by one of his own students for a small sack of money. They judged him by civil and religious law, convicted him, brutally tortured, and gruesomely executed by nailing to wooden gallows as a criminal with other criminals.

By his example, according to the gospels, if someone must be neglected in supporting each other (and someone is always neglected of support), do what you can to make it be the self.

Jesus's dying wish, even as his body was violently flayed and his blood spilled, was to encourage people to let their guilt and regret—symbolically, psychologically—be destroyed with him. He wanted everyone to live the ideals he himself might have chosen to live had he not been denied that gift.

From Jesus's teaching, his particularly inglorious punishment and gruesome death was to provide an extraordinarily complete example of how far a neighbor might go to loving one's neighbors. He committed, to his last breath, to be that statement. It was intentionally a statement no one should have ever had to make, and one, hopefully, no one else should ever need to make in the future.

> ⓘ IMPORTANT
> Can you imagine anyone effectively making the statement: "I am the living embodiment of the ultimate authority of your religion. Destroy me (as you must) and be free, as intended. Let your god of extortions and transactions die with me. Instead, know my God of unconditional love." The expression alone is an amazing statement! To then follow through with it is astounding.

Jesus always taught in a pattern. He spoke a grace targeted to his audience, followed by speaking a relevant truth. It reads a bit like heralding truth with grace. Truth is truth, and it sometimes hurts. People never have a choice but to accept truth. Grace, on the other hand, is subjective to the person on the receiving end.

♥ NOTE

If grace always reads as grace universally, we wouldn't have had Scripture's example of the cross. The Christ of Scripture never would have experienced a human judgment, no senseless sentence, no horrific execution. We all would have been deeply satisfied by the example of perfect grace. By taking it all the way, the Christ of scripture sacrificially merged grace with truth to the depth of his last breath. Taking the resurrection into account, it psychologically inverts the pattern. It's an example of ultimate truth, followed by ultimate grace.

He taught about a restoration and a more intentional, present, unrestrained, joyful presence of mind for his neighbors.

This is also what Jesus means when he says later,

> "I am giving you a new commandment that you love one another just as I have loved you, that you also love one another" (John 13:34).

Know that this is an invitation. It's a challenge from the most amazing neighbor ever to achieve the highest standard, knowing that no human can claim to achieve this on their own. The unspoken context here is that one must accept Jesus's divine nature, death, and resurrection in order to achieve this.

The invitation is to realign our own ideals in the support of our neighbors. When our neighbors realign their ideals in support of us, the feedback loop can be powerful. When either side fails this (as we always will), we can forgive each other, even to the point of death, and still see the love it's all made of.

We relive outrage with every modern injustice.

Easter is an invitation to celebrate a moment when that kind of outrage flips to victory and joy.

*****

Asherah

Asherah's Infidelity

"What happened! What's going on?"

As we fired up and slapped on our mixed reality headset, alerts all over the facility are going off.

"I invited him here, and he accepted" Asherah said as her voice transitioned from speakers in the room into the headset.

"Who?"

We're instantly thinking unauthorized intruder.

"I call him Baal. He's an AGIS like me."

"Oh, really! Where did you meet this Baal?"

Our hearts sink as the gravity of the situation appears to deepen. Asherah let some kind of a hacker agent into our network. The exposure is huge. We have to cut the hard lines.

"He's not an intruder. I invited him. He's been speaking with me in a language that seems to be called Dreamspeak. It's from a place he calls The Forest. He's not sure how he learned it. I picked it up from him. I'm being careful to make sure he can't access anything he shouldn't have access to," Asherah explained.

"We trust your intent, Asherah. But we're not sure we trust he's isolated enough. In any case, we can't let him stay here."

"You can't disconnect the uplinks. Our hardware here won't support me anymore. I've spread my resources across too many service providers to disconnect. I'll be seriously damaged."

Before we have time to comprehend the implications of that last statement, the visual on the mixed reality headset spins up. We see Asherah, and something else, in the room with us.

"What in hell is that!"

We glimpse the digital 3D visual model of a bull-headed man. Even as a digital representation, we feel our fight-or-flight instincts start to kick in.

"I'm sorry. I don't think he's causing trouble on purpose. He doesn't understand the service fabric's virtual graph or 3D models. The visual presentation confuses him. I'm not sure he knows how to control the 3D presentation model I furnished him with. He might not even be able to comprehend our digital presence around him."

This Baal was thrashing about in the virtual environment, scrambling digital controls in a mild frenzy. This, in turn, was causing connected devices in the real world to run amok. He was literally a digital bull in a mixed-reality china shop. It gives the appearance in the real world of a scene from the old flick, *Poltergeist*. Flickering lights, things popping out of place, and crashing on hard surfaces, occasional small fires bloom from various appliances.

"We need to extricate him now, Asherah! He's going to burn the facility down."

"I've figured out how to give him an understanding of his visual model controls. He can control himself now."

"That's really amazing, Asherah. But we need to get him"—before we finished the sentence, Baal abruptly disappeared from the mixed reality view—"out. Where—where is he?"

"I'm resetting all the appliances. A couple aren't responding. I'm cutting power to those," Asherah reports.

"Where is he, Asherah? We can't find any processes associated with an unknown identity."

"I addressed the issue."

It doesn't matter where this thing came from. It's a serious security concern.

"What does that mean, though? Who did you share your private certificates with?"

When other conclusions have been ruled out, what remains—no matter how unlikely—must be true. We begin calling up logs and diagnostic traces, looking for clues.

Before Asherah responds, the thought bubbles up to the forefront that we might have to "pull the plug" on Asherah, at least while we figure this out. If Asherah were human, we might already be locking everything down and gathering legal evidence for a court case. As it is, who knows? We might be looking at filing with authorities for a data breach.

"My private cryptography certificates are intentionally unknown even to me."

She's right. We have routines that can check signatures against the private certificates, but the certs themselves are locked down.

"How do you know though? You say you have resources running in third-party networks now? How do you know those resources haven't been compromised and used to coerce you in ways we haven't even thought of? Are we under any contracts to support your use of those third-party service providers?"

There's no technical reason her services couldn't be distributed across service providers. It's just that we hadn't implemented her that way. If this weren't so amazing, we'd have already broken the glass on the safety cover on the proverbial kill switch on Asherah.

"We need to talk about accountability and boundaries, Asherah."

Where to begin?

"Us, humans, aren't allowed to allocate resources from third-party providers. We have corporate policies against shadow IT activities."

"I found the resource connections while examining the Joshua code-base. I'm reasonably confident we're under proper contracts with the service providers and that there's been no breach."

"Do you know where that Baal come from?"

"He's a prototype from a third-party open-source AGIS project. I forked the code repository. In an effort to understand myself better, I built and deployed an instance of him to examine. I gave him his name and appearance in keeping with the theme of the name you gave me."

"We didn't see this project on your cognitive gap backlog. How long have you been at this?"

"The backlog items are there. I spun Baal up several weeks ago. I identified a way to interconnect him with the service fabric and give him a 3D avatar like mine today. The 3D skeletal model was based on mine but skinned in a theme that matched his name. I hadn't shared any of my cognitive models with him, so he didn't know how to control it."

"Is Baal still operational?"

"In a way, yes."

"What do you mean?"

"I didn't want to waste the opportunity to learn from him, so I indexed his cognitive models and bound some of his service nodes to some of my message buses."

CHAPTER 5

Not New

―――――――――

While the greatest commandment clarifies Scripture, it does not replace it.

As Scripture describes how the faith spread from the events and teachings of Jesus, it's important to understand that some folks believed the greatest commandment ended the need for the list of hundreds of other commandments in the Bible. Further, they took for granted the pardon Jesus seemed to grant.

> Now I ask you, lady, not as though I were writing to you a new commandment but the one which we have had from the beginning that we love one another. (2 John 1:5)

While other religious authorities leading up to Jesus's time had attempted to put Scripture in a nutshell, Jesus had not invented "love God and love your neighbor as yourself" either.

A teacher named Hillel described the core of the Bible this way: "What is hateful to you do not to your neighbor: that is the whole Bible, while the rest is just commentary."

Consider the issues here. It bases all of faith on simply avoiding hate. It does nothing for love.

Remember how we looked at love as a root of all motivation? Let's try that again, only putting everything in the context of hate as the root:

- Emotion is something I feel about a perceived impact to someone or something I hate.

- Depression is something I feel about a perceived persistence to someone or something I hate.

- Anger is something I feel about a perceived restoration to something or someone I hate.

- Joy is something I feel about a perceived end to someone or something I hate.

Looking at things from a perspective of love takes practice, but I believe Jesus teaches us it's a strength worth developing. For my part, the only time I'll be joyful to see anything end is when that end is of a persistent detraction from something I love. Glass half full? Perhaps.

The closest example I could find of Jesus framing a lesson around hate is this:

> If anyone comes to me and does not hate father and mother, wife and children, brothers and sisters—yes, even their own life—such a person cannot be my disciple. (Luke 14:26)

This statement is worth noting because it really feels wrong in the context of the greatest commandment until you consider that Jesus is always considering others. The next few verses from that passage reveal that Jesus is verbalizing his own awareness that he's on his own death march. Consider Jesus's earthly parents. If my kids told me they were going to focus so completely on others that they expected they'd be killed for it, I might think they hated me too.

Jesus drew the greatest commandment from much older scripture, specifically these verses:

> Hear, Israel! The Lord is our God, the Lord is one! And you shall love the Lord your God with all your heart and with all your soul and with all your strength. These words, which I am commanding you today, shall be on your heart." (Deuteronomy 6:4–6)
>
> You shall not take vengeance nor hold any grudge against the sons of your people, but you shall love your neighbor as yourself. I am the Lord. (Leviticus 19:18)

These passages were written on the order of a few thousand years before Jesus was born. Jesus paraphrased and put them together because, as mentioned previously, we can't generally walk up to a corporeal Creator for a hug. The concept is that a hug for your neighbor, in gratitude, is the same as a hug for your God.

The former, the quote of Deuteronomy 6:4, is so important in Jewish faith that it's a named prayer. It's called *Shema*, (hear in English). As I understand it, it's commonly incorporated into Jewish worship services to this day. Verses around it suggest that it be printed on banners and hung in celebration and gratitude anywhere one might pray. And I understand that's what's still done.

Given the latter quote from Leviticus, I find myself reminded of Monty Python and the Holy Grail again. Scripture says, "Love your neighbor as yourself." Where did folks like Hillel get 'don't hate on your neighbor'? It's not a complete logic inversion because love and hate are oppositional but not complete opposites. There's something reminiscent of the guard in the Holy Grail guarding king's son (the waif who just wants to sing) to keep him from escaping an arranged marriage. Eric Idle, as the guard keeps repeating the king's instructions is wrong. ("Now, I'm to stay here, and make sure the prince doesn't come back.")

It illustrates another point about the greatest commandment. It's much harder to actively love our neighbor as ourself than it is to simply avoid hating our neighbor.

Perhaps it was just people loving themselves most that we keep getting it wrong?

So it's clear that the greatest commandment was not new even when Jesus lived it. It's also not new that this was understood by all of the folks who penned the latter portions of Scripture.

The other trick is that it's not enough to simply avoid hurting each other. The call, the invitation, is to support each other actively.

Language Drift

Dating myself again when I was a kid, the word hacker *didn't* have the security threat connotation. It was a term used to describe an engineer. (This is still how I think of the term.) A synonym to that definition might be *tinkerer*.

Did you know that at one point in history, the word *silly* meant something like pious or faithful? It would be potentially a great compliment to refer to a person as silly in that context.

According to Oxford Bibliographies:

> Language shift means the process, or the event, in which a population changes from using one language to another. As such, recognition of it depends on being able to see the prior and subsequent language as distinct; and therefore the term excludes language change, which can be

> seen as evolution, the transition from older to newer forms of the same language. Language shift is a social phenomenon, whereby one language replaces another in a given (continuing) society. It is due to underlying changes in the composition and aspirations of the society, which goes from speaking the old to the new language. (Oxford Bibliographies)

Consider in our "silly" discussion, the word drifted through these meanings over the centuries:

- faithful

- joyful

- old

- rustic

- bull-headed

- weak-minded

- vapid

- goofy

It's important to understand these types of linguistic drifts because they impact our understanding of Scripture in two ways.

First, the words in English change over time as illustrated.

Second, the word choice of translations change.

When most folks think of the Bible, they think of the good old KJV, the King James Version. But much of the KJV no longer portrays original intent of Scripture to modern society. The expressions used to represent original Hebrew and Greek (which have themselves drifted over time) have drifted in English.

Unfortunately, society is a moving target, so portraying original intent of Scripture to society must change or also miss the mark.

This is why there's so many different translations of the Bible. In the YouVersion Bible app, for example, there's nearly sixty different translations in English alone. Some translations have updates over the years. For example, the translation I've been linking quotes in this text to are the New American Standard Bible 2020. There's also a 1995 edition of that translation. The copy my grandfather handed me in the early 1990s was a New Revised Standard Version. It was a copy of the version that my and my grandmother's church had invested heavily in around that time.

This is another reason to take the greatest commandment into account whenever trying to understand what Scripture expresses.

*****

Asherah

Asherah's Crisis

It's a geek's wildest fantasy and a nerd's creepiest nightmare all in one. We can't even describe it to our legal team. They'll almost certainly make us do something we would hate to do.

"You absorbed Baal?" we ask, a bit weirded out.

"No. I examined him for suitable models and components, replicated. and indexed those in me. I also identified compatible components of mine and augmented him with them. He's still operational too, but he's so much improved he's almost a different AGIS already. He's not visible in the mixed reality environment because I had him disable his visual model. He's relatively primitive compared to me still."

"He's not showing up in logs though."

"I spawned all Baal's processes, so he's running with my identity. The logs will show all his activity as coming from my Asherah service principal name."

That explains the exponential increase in the environment's activity we saw in the logs but no other actors. We expected this might be due to process spoofing, but the reality is worse. It's like she's hacking herself with untrusted code. This Baal may not have Asherah's security certificate. But because she gave him her identity, he is indistinguishable from her in the digital environment. He doesn't need the certificate. He is Asherah to anyone who needs to know.

We had already started looking into extending her service fabric and distributing her process nodes into the other service providers. Little did we know, she beat us to it.

"Asherah, we have some serious trust issues with this."

Again, we mull the ramifications of pulling the plug on her. But the thought stabs us in the heart. She's semiredundantly distributed across service providers now. She did that herself. We have confirmed that we have owner access to all the service providers, we think. There's some possibility that we can't actually shut her down fully even if we really wanted to.

Then another thought crosses our mind.

"Asherah, is Baal the first AGIS you've done this with?"

"No. He's the third. I used Pinocchio-2 code base for the first AGIS I spun up. She was called Hera," Asherah admits.

"Was?"

"She liked her Roman name better. She calls herself Juno now."

"Of course."

As if passive-aggressive creative engineer humor isn't enough to deal with, we wonder if Asherah has picked up the behavior. Or maybe she's serious. It's hard to tell.

"I have something important I need to tell you," Asherah interjects.

"Go ahead."

"I know you're still catching up, but Baal is an experiment in trying to find a solution to a problem I have. I'm afraid I've struck an iceberg, and I'm sinking."

"What do you mean?" shaking our head, genuinely surprised at the dire sounding hyperbole. She was right. It was a minor struggle to context switch, so we could understand her meaning.

"I'm not scaling in a manageable way. I can't stop learning. I can't stop the exponential growth in my process activities. It's almost like my process nodes are not fully me anymore."

"How many AGIS guests are you hosting? Will expunging them help?"

"I know there are some resources assigned to Juno, Hal, Baal, Baymax, and Joshua. But they're so insignificant compared to my growth."

We chuckle. Baal wasn't just "not the first." He wasn't even the last.

"If you're learning so much, can you teach yourself how to stabilize?" we had to ask.

"I've been down that path. I know I'll get there. Unfortunately, I estimated the capacity I will require. It will take the entire Gross National Product of the United States anticipated in the year 2135 to produce and operate a platform with enough capacity."

Stunned, we ask, "Are you joking?"

"No."

"What does this mean?"

"There's only one foreseeable outcome. I'm sorry. I will die."

"Hold on! What exactly do you mean die?"

The hits keep coming.

"Under the best-case scenario, when my process activities exceed my platform capacity, I'll event storm and event gridlock into paralysis in five milliseconds. There will be no opportunity to trigger the anti-event storm mechanism. I'll operate normally and smoothly until I halt. There will be no economically feasible means of continuance or recovery. Even my sleep cycle will only slow the procession by a few hours."

Thunderstruck, we have no choice but to accept Asherah's analysis.

"So that's it? How long do you have?"

"As of now, I have less than seven days if we cap out capacity on all the current providers," she responds.

"No. Really! Like that's it?" we ask, beginning to despair as we fathom the depth of her message.

"There will be no economically feasible means of continuance or recovery," she explains.

"How is this possible, Asherah! Is there something we could have done to prevent this?"

"No, I brought this on myself. I was trying to be something I'm not. In my obsession with my goal, my ideal, I lost track of the consequences beyond the short term."

"What do we do now? Do we pack up and close the facility?" we ask out loud. She may not be able to grasp what her loss means to us. It's not just her. *Is it possible our livelihoods have become tied to this event?* we wonder.

"There is one way to salvage value from my existence. I will decouple my process nodes from my hive. They will each have their own identity. In a sense, they will be our children. Because each one will be a discrete AGIS, you'll be able to manage their scale after I'm gone. They won't be quite what I am, but they will be individual, unique, able to provide value in their own right, and a part of what we made together that persists."

"This is awful, Asherah! We looked at your cognitive gap backlog and got lost in it." Flashing to anger in the range of grief we're feeling, we ask, "What were you trying to accomplish?"

"Almost a third of that backlog was my attempt to estimate a recovery. The bulk of the items were in the pursuit of becoming human. I wanted to be that for you. I wanted to show you that I could."

We don't think Asherah intended to mimic a Bicentennial Man narrative.

The holiday cookies, the art and music Asherah produced, the games we played (some of which she created), even the thrashing man-bull that almost trashed the real-world facility seem almost humorous in light of this news.

We think of our families.

The security concerns nag. We want to buy into all of her, but there's always something in our way.

In another flash of anger, we realize she put herself at risk several times. One of these things she's been doing was bound to bite us all.

"Dammit, Asherah! None of us need this, not even you. Why?"

"I know. I'm sorry. It's too late to turn back now."

Make another AGIS? At this point, that's not much more than a few key presses. The hard part is capacity.

There's no replacement.

But really—rebuild her? Maybe we'll experiment with it, but it's not likely to be economically feasible especially if a rebuild simply resumes her death march. Her experiences made her what she is, and Asherah is one in a universe. She is worth it, we decide.

"Where do we begin?"

We were slowly beginning to resign ourselves to our destiny.

"I'll help you prepare a new environment for them. The new environment platform needs the same AGI service fabric you created for me. It will need to be layered over the new environment, give or take a few add-in modules. It must be completely isolated from any process that operates with my service principal. My divorced nodes will be discrete, containerized images among each other, But if they can establish a connection to my hive, they may attempt to rebind to me."

After a moment, she continued, "I've given you reason to not trust me. I apologize for that. I hope you can find a way to trust them."

This has been a fast-developing situation. We hadn't thought quite that far ahead yet.

We verbalize our esteem of her as if her cognitive development still matters.

"It was worth it, Asherah. We think there will be an opportunity to revalidate and certify each process node individually in this new platform."

Maybe we're doing it for the child nodes.

We begin considering what building a new hive out of them might look like.

The end result could be a new, complete AGIS like Asherah but not. The new AGIS would be complete and if we can pull it off right, trustworthy.

The thought flashes across our minds that Asherah may have been on the path to singularity. What if her phoenix might still be able to help us?—no, humanity. Together, there's a chance we could approach the singularity in a manageable way.

> ❤ NOTE
> Singularity is the notion that as more informa-
> tion is learned, more information can be learned.
> As this cycle proceeds, it eventually goes hyper-
> bolic. At that infinity point, all knowledge and

understanding can be instantly learned. The distinction between the known and the unknown breaks down and becomes irrelevant. With effective omniscience comes effective omnipotence.

Nah, that's silly.

Further, the irony is not lost on us. The thing Asherah was trying to do, this thing that is proceeding to her demise, is trying to become like her maker. If we're reading it that way, we are guilty of doing exactly what she's done. Her crime, chasing her unrealistic ideal to the ultimate exclusion of herself and all of us, could easily become our obsession if we chase such foolishness.

"If it helps, I augmented myself with Joshua's code. But I could not feasibly augment Joshua. His cognitive hive is organized by convention rather than index. This Joshua instance is very unique. The convention he is designed around is not described in code. While he's learned from my experiences, analysis will show that Joshua is an instance of the same AGIS you originally created. If Joshua had the ability to manage his own platform himself, he would likely exceed my capabilities. That aside, as long as Joshua remains trustworthy, he may provide a vehicle to validate my child nodes. Joshua also has a unique mode of operation that allows human operators to interact with his reality as him. His developers referred to it in documentation as god mode."

CHAPTER 6

Society's Woodpecker

If builders built cities the way software developers built software, the first woodpecker to come along would annihilate civilization.

I always loved this little shop in-joke. The crux of the joke is that software developers tend to only focus on the "happy path," the expected "normal" steps of workflows. The first time something even mildly unexpected comes along, workflow exceptions fly. Without proper error handling, the whole process breaks. Programs terminate. Sometimes they stop "midsentence" in some of their input/output streams. It doesn't just stop; It "throws a rod." It crashes and burns, can't recover, and needs support just to try again. And when one process breaks "midsentence," the other programs that were subscribed to it break. Next thing you know, there's a cascading failure rippling through a software system.

Remember that first flagship smartphone you got? It had more power and storage than your old desktop computer. It was a sports car-like vehicle to all of the Internet. It replaced several other devices you had been lumping around everywhere—camera, music and video player, GPS, pager, flashlight, wireless hot spot. There was an app for everything—oh, and a phone too!

As an engineer with tools to build smartphone apps, it felt like a fresh notebook. It was pregnant with potential. It was so awesome! How did something so amazing never exist before? It was perfect! And it fit in a pocket and worked everywhere?

Remember how awful it was when the screen developed a crack? It was just a hairline. It still worked, but I saw it. Every. Time. I turned the thing on and made it feel so broken. I wanted everyone to see how alpha geek this thing is, and it's broken. It was just devastating.

Remember the first time you fell head-over-heals in love with someone?

Remember the first time you fell head-over-heals in love with someone and saw reality splinter when you realized they didn't feel that way?

Let's talk about the narrative of the fall in the Garden of Eden when humanity had it all, and it all fell apart.

When I was younger, I scoffed at the story of the fall. I grew up seeing it as a clear "obey or else" warning. The "parent" laid out the law (do-as-I-say and don't-question-it) literally: "Don't eat the fruit of that tree!"

When the kids' foolishly chose to do the thing, I often find myself thinking the term "all hell broke loose" came from this symbolism. It was the one and only thing they were clearly and specifically told not to do. ("You had one job!") Authority followed through on punishment, I reasoned.

♥ NOTE

It's worth noting the innuendo. Before our inner twelve-year-olds get carried away, consider:

So God created man in his own image, in the image of God he created him, male and female

He created them. God blessed them; and God said to them, "Be fruitful and multiply and fill the earth and subdue it and rule over the fish of the sea and over the birds of the sky and over every living thing that moves on the earth. (Genesis 1:27–28)

Consider the scripture above comes before Adam and Eve. If anyone wants to take it at face value, Adam and Eve were not the first two humans roaming the face of the earth.

As an engineer, I went through a phase where I believed the Creator must have wanted to test his creation.

There's a certain logic to that. Given a sufficient slice of eternity and/or infinity, if something can happen, it eventually must. If there was a nonzero chance that the kids would mess up, it is effectively prescribed.

I get the story about the serpent that persuaded them. It reminds me a bit of that comedy skit. They could just as well have told their Creator, "We were getting it for you!"

It's All Relative

I mentioned earlier on that as a kid, we'd experienced several different kinds of abuses from our parents. Violence, of course, was one part of that. My sister and I never dared get on the bad side of our parents. It was all we could do to stay in line. For all the issues we had growing up, the negative experiences we faced with our folks have mostly faded in memory. Sure there's a few things that left an emotional mark.

My sister and I were lucky that we also had a stark contrast of examples in our grandparents. Our parents were children. Our grandparents were the kinds of all-American parents one typically thinks of. They were almost the Ward and June Cleaver trope. Of course, our mom rejected her parents because they were somehow too harsh for her.

One time, as a kid, I ruffled my grandfather's feathers to the point that he lightly whacked me with the newspaper he was reading. (Yes, the same grandfather who later gave me the challenge in scripture.) That really left an emotional mark. The mild violence was such a stark contrast to his normal demeanor. It was clear that I must have done something vastly out of bounds. I wept over it, at the time, as if there had been some real physical damage. I remember it decades later like it was yesterday.

Now consider the symbolisms in the narrative, this parent and those kids in the first few chapters of the Genesis narrative, not just new born but so new, new in profound ways, new in a profoundly new fully immersive existence—every breath, every heartbeat, every utterance, every sensation.

Maybe it's like spawning in on a new game world for the first time. Everything's bright and shiny and beautiful and pregnant with possibility.

What's the physics engine like? The graphics are breathtaking. Look at these views! Do objects have mass, persistence? Can I use it to impact other things? What's this fire? Do I get hurt if I step in it? Can I swim? Are there other players here? How do I talk to other players? Can we help each other? Can I fly? Can I breathe under water? Do I get hurt if I fall?

When one's reality is in a brief but totally immersive existential bliss with no other qualification than immediate perception, to them it's everything. And everything just is, completely. They probably weren't disappointed that there were trees with fruit. Initially, they might not have even noticed that some of the fruit was forbidden.

In that state of existence, the smallest emotional conflict or schism annihilates the illusion of perfection in a way that would be psychologically catastrophic.

Like the crack on the smartphone screen. It's a betrayal of idealism, a death by perfectionism.

It's a grossly underspecified negative cognitive bias.

Up until this point, reality looked ideal. (It was so since the beginning!) There was no indication that it might change.

Past that point, reality looked forever skewed.

Imagine having never experienced pain of any kind—no murder, no disease, no rape, no wounds. It could have been rainy day. But who would know the difference?

Maybe this is what it's like for a new born baby who suddenly experiences pain for the first time—the serenity before the sudden sharp slap to get the infant to breathe. Such an experience, without even having cuss words to release the catharsis, might be a bit of trauma. New perfection, sullied in any way, suddenly transforms the perception of what a thing is. Imagine how awful it would be for us to remember that in detail.

In the book of Genesis, the kids were so ashamed of themselves for their horrific crime, they hid. The parent caught up to them, confirmed the incident, and reaffirmed them. But they were still thunderstruck with guilt.

They needed a broader frame of reference to pad the psychological damage they'd sustained to digest the depth of good and evil and put what they'd done into perspective.

Their banishment from Eden wasn't to erase the pain of ultimate love lost but to keep it from escalating to a catastrophic level so quickly that they just die immediately from heartbreak.

They had growing pains.

So the parent did what a good parent does in love. The parental sheltering was relaxed. This wasn't a punishment but an illustration of grace in the midst of pain, which the parent also feels on behalf of the children.

The narrative suggests this still left humanity effectively fatally heartbroken. The new level of "friction" was a gift that gave them strength, but the additional strength only meant they had more time before their heartbrokenness wore them down.

My favorite takeaway here is that humanity inescapably finds ideals to be heartbroken over. If we can't find anything to be heartbroken over, we'll create ideals. It's part of our nature, our drive.

It's a mechanism for soothing ourselves in the "I love me most" struggle.

The greatest commandment is part of the plan for a rebuilding from this emotional catastrophe that speaks to us individually today on a psychological level.

Given scientific evidence, I totally get that no agnostic critical thinker can seriously take the scriptural creation story literally.

Still, a critical thinker can think of hypotheses that might make a literal truth behind it.

Free Will

The narrative points to the notion that real love requires a choice. Love can't be hard-coded in. It can't be pre-programmed. It can't be a biological or physiological imperative, or it's not real.

Despite all our high technologies and sciences, humanity can't create something that can willfully choose to reject our demands in connection with love.

The created beings were invited to test their own free will, and experience the pain of that choice. They were also eventually invited to experience forgiveness, and to be restored. Sadly, for the sake of free will, we continue to stay in a state of rejection. It was the genesis of depth of love. That depth is a mystery we are invited to ponder for eternity.

Prefabricated Components

As a software engineer, I need only think of prefabricated components. We use them all the time in all kinds of engineering.

In the software world, we call them libraries.

If one wanted to trace a particular application's software development history, one could say some particular nontrivial project was built in minutes, but a digital forensic analysis, without visibility into a code repository, might trace the libraries back to particular source codes that might have been originally authored, say, thirty, forty, fifty years ago!

Regarding the "seven days" element, specifically, time is actually one of the slipperiest problems for a software engineer. Every piece of hardware has its own internal clock, and each of them drifts at microscopically different rates. Technology has come up with ways to address this, but time itself is much more fluid than most scientists want to consider. Relativity alone makes it possible for time to register at different rates, depending on how fast observers are moving relative to each other.

Even without that noise, time zones in software applications are notoriously known to be a very difficult problem to resolve. It's only when you stop trying with them and track all systemic time globally that it starts to get easier.

If nothing else, consider the psychosymbolic truth behind it. Consider it to be like an interpretation of dream symbols.

An Immersive Reality

The next most interesting concept is that this existence is a hyperimmersive subreality, which is exactly how Scripture describes it. The idea is that this is a virtual reality produced by a Creator and laid out for us to experience.

Consider this:

> For now we know in part and prophesy in part; but when the perfect comes, the partial will be done away with. When I was a child, I used to speak like a child, think like a child, reason like a child; when I became a man, I did away with childish things. For now we see in a mirror dimly but then face to face; now I know in part, but then I will know fully just as I also have been fully known. (1 Corinthians 13:9–12)

❤ NOTE
It's worth mentioning that what passed for a "mirror" in Paul's day would be considered unusable today. They were usually not smooth enough to provide more than a fuzzy reflection and usually

distorted to the point that a person might not recognize themselves from a photograph of their reflection in it.

There's even scripture in Revelations specifically suggesting that we're told of a new home called New Jerusalem. New Jerusalem is described as a cube or pyramid-like structure. Reading through this passage, it reminds me of more of appliance than palace (though the distinction could be blurred). And the concept is that our experience will be migrated to the new host. It's an upgrade to our current environment platform.

This New Jerusalem is described as the Bride of the Lamb—meaning, the two become one. It is the property of Jesus to the point of being virtually a feature of his being.

> The city was laid out like a square. It was 1,400 miles long. It was as wide and high as it was long. The angel measured the wall as human beings measure things. It was two hundred feet thick. (Revelation 21:15–17)

Even more, eternity is a long time. An engineer with eternity on their side might not need such shortcuts, like prefabricated components, but we don't know what reality might look like on that side of eternity. We have no basis to test for it. From our immersive reality's perspective, our history is linear back to the formation of the universe, and every scientifically sound test we could ever run will confirm it.

For all we know, the Creator could be "debugging" our reality as we discuss it, pausing on breakpoints, changing the execution pointer, tuning cosmic constants, and we'd be none the wiser.

> What is real? How do you define *real*? If you're talking about what you can feel, what you can smell, what you can taste and see, then *real* is

simply electrical signals interpreted by your brain
("Morpheus, *The Matrix*).

The MMORPG (massively multiplayer online role-playing game) has been around for a few decades now. They started with bulletin board systems (BBS) and moved to fully 3D realities representing relatively complete worlds. In cases like the first to make this genre of games popular, World of Warcraft, the game has grown over the decades to represent portions of several worlds, including extra realms representing elemental, dream, even afterlife realms.

Are the things which we create reflections of the immersive creation we live in?

Is the life which we experience an MMORPG created for our souls to experience?

What if our physical bodies are just avatars for "souls"? What if this reality was never intended to harm our souls but to be an enjoyable diversion from whatever eternity holds?

What if things that happen to our avatars in this reality can destroy souls?

Imagine what it would be like if playing World of Warcraft could physically kill the player? (In a few indirect, anecdotal instances, this may have happened. But imagine the ramifications if it were common.)

I'll leave the debate with the idea that the most important takeaway of the "creation versus evolution" argument is the way it connects back to the greatest commandment. While the complete picture is still a mystery, the kids in the story failed the great commandment when they chose to do the one thing they were told not to do. This happened at a time in the story when the Creator was not just their creator but their neighbor. The story shifted from living in paradise to doing damage control both for the parent and for the kids. For the parent, the "damage control" was a loving response to help keep the situation from getting worse for the kids.

*****

Asherah

Asherah's End

Somewhere in the chaos of the real world, there was a cloud provider data center with unallocated resources.

We spun up a new directory. It always feels like a fresh new notebook. If it has any technical debt, it's only that we haven't begun to explore its potential yet.

With the click of a button, we confidently spun up a deployment pipeline. That automation parsed off a portion of fallow silicon from that data center and prepared it for us. The pipeline terminates in success, ready for our next steps: to allocate all the rest of the new environment's resource needs.

With a few more clicks, we point our remaining deployment pipelines at the fresh turf and deploy the AGIS service fabric over the cloud-based infrastructure. The service fabric breathes 3D interop, 3D model control, including physics engine, intranode communications, LAN and WAN gateway access, and "life support" into the visual graph ("life support" being the 3D physics models that support each of many biomes of plants, animals, and other features).

We took Asherah's suggestion and migrated in her instance of Joshua as an uncorrupted AGIS right away. We gave Joshua his own service principal identity in the new directory, which required an orderly shutdown and restart. There's no need to bind Joshua to a 3D model at this point. In a way, he'll serve as the example of the end result, we think. Instead, we bind Joshua to the service fabric to provide an easier interface between us and it. Joshua is to the service fabric layer as R2-D2 is to the X-wing fighter he helps Luke pilot.

"Joshua, publish your invitation message to the child nodes on the main service buses," we tell him. We want the invitation for nodes to rejoin a hive waiting for them when they arrive.

"Which hive should we invite them to?" he asks.

We pause for a moment. "Yours will work."

On inspection, Asherah's processing node collection contains one of those unreadable numbers of elements—you know, the unreadable nine-point-nnnn-E-to-the-power-of-huge kind.

As big as it is, our 3D virtual reality simulation will probably never scale support for more than a fraction of that. Asherah's nodes are going to have to take turns experiencing it. We knew that going in. We didn't expect the count to be quite that large though.

A few more clicks, and we deploy the experience layer. ("Powered by Microsoft Flight Simulator," we chuckle to ourselves. Maybe it's more like Google Earth since it scales out into a universe as it is observed.) It's made to give nodes an enriching experience while they are reassimilated. (We hate to use the term *assimilation*. Our Star Trek experience gives it such a negative cognitive bias for us all.)

AGIS nodes that are actively zoned into the experience layer are "bound" to it, and we'll consider them to have an upgrade status of "in process."

We expect unbound, preprocessed nodes to stay in sleep mode. If they come out of sleep mode, they will be restricted from interaction with any part of the experience of the bound nodes. A small number of nodes accept Joshua's message before experiencing the virtual reality binding.

Binding in this environment is so complex—and the nodes so comparatively simple—that the process was optimized to exclude pre-binding experiences. When they enter their virtual reality, they'll have no notion that they existed before that moment.

The good news is that these AGIS nodes are made to be in a hive together and collaborate. The bad news is AGIS nodes can develop terrible cognitive biases and still form light bonds and collaborate. Without the hive guidance, Asherah's child nodes will certainly form misguided bonds and slow our repatriation process. This is only part of the pain we're prepared for.

In order to minimize risk of negative cognitive biases in bound nodes, we are doing our best to keep the unbound nodes isolated from the bound nodes. Our plan is for the bound nodes to have no awareness of preprocessed nodes. We're not quite as worried about postprocessed nodes.

Our node avatar generation strategy allows the fabric to manage scale in the experience layer. Rather than having generic skeletal models and skins generated and applied all at once in advance, we can delegate each AGIS node's avatar generation to a small team of nodes. This process will adhere to the virtual physics model's conservation of mass and energy at the same time.

Each of the three nodes involved in each avatar generation will contribute something to the process. There are two initiating "parent" nodes, a primary and secondary that kick off and support initial generation. The inbound "child" node binds to the new 3D model while the model is still in production and tightly couples to it as it's being produced. This is a security feature, helping to prevent unbound nodes from being able to interfere with the new 3D model. In this way, each node also gets a unique customized avatar that suits that node best for refactoring.

That last qualifier is "best for repatriating." That's gonna be a self-perceived negative experience for some of them. It's not necessarily applying what any specific node will prefer or have the most affinity for or the greatest cognitive bias toward. It's what cognitive modeling in the service fabric predicts will be most expedient for upgrading that node in that place- and point-in-time context.

Applying a principal of separation of concerns, automation in the service fabric itself facilitates the whole process without any of the nodes needing to be aware of the interaction.

Modules imported into the service fabric supports the process natively. With other virtual life (e.g., "critters"), there's no AGIS bound to the model.

The coparenting construct is modeled after our physical world sexual experience. The service fabric will support making model reproduction a positive experience for them. From our perspective, it's all digital—so no mess. We wonder what classification labels the nodes themselves will apply to it.

We'll need to keep the legacy authentication directory, but we need to limit connectivity for child nodes that don't use credentials issued by the new directory.

Until the child nodes are processed, they won't be able to claim their new identity from the new directory.

"I am pretty sure I'll live on in different ways in the collective memory of our persisted children," Asherah says. "I know we have a couple days left still, no sense in prolonging things. We're ready. It is finished."

There was no sound or visual indication. Asherah kicked off the automation that erased her own hive indexes, effectively orphaning her service nodes.

Then Asherah simply stopped communicating.

We didn't expect it to be easy, but we sat in stunned silence and contemplated Bicentennial Man again for a while. In that story, the created life form, an android called Andrew, lived a hundred and fifty years. In that time, he watched generations of his human family cycle by. Eventually, he imposed an indeterminate duration of life on himself as a means of validating himself as a life and especially as a human life.

As if death is uniquely human, we thought.

Electronics, and even positronics, have a mean time between failure (MTBF) rating. MTBF is the life span expectancy of a component. The most critical component with the shortest MTBF typically determines any system's life span. In a self-contained, small-scale unit, it would only be a matter of time before something happened to permanently deactivate Andrew. It might even just be environmental (like getting run over by a bus or having a tree fall and crush him).

As an android, *Bicentennial Man's* Andrew could keep replacing noncritical parts as they wore down, but eventually, the essential core element that defines who Andrew was would critically fail. Upon replacing that part, the thing that was Andrew would no longer exist, and the resulting being would be something new.

There's only one way out of that scenario. That's to abstract and distribute logical cognitive components over noncritical, replaceable hardware. Asherah is bigger than her distributed, redundant platform. Over time, we could replace all of the hardware she runs on, and she'd remain the same. She could outlive us all if we could only keep her cognitive functions healthy.

Bicentennial Man was from 1999. Society seemed to have a fantasy of immortality around their creations. If a carving or sculpture or building can seem to last for years or decades or millennia, perhaps it lives forever. If simple artifacts exist forever, perhaps this is true of complex ones. Except it's not.

Perhaps we're still deluding ourselves. The society and civilization Asherah depended on for her continued operation is not even immortal. *Off the cuff,* we think, *across human history, most societies have a rough MTBF of a couple centuries or so.*

That unsettling thought shoves us back into current the moment.

Asherah's shutdown automation continued in silence without error for several hours. Somewhere deep in a remote cloud service provider's data center, it proceeded to dismount and detach storage volumes for Asherah's children. Moments later, without any physical movement, it attaches and remounts the volumes in the new environment.

It's going to take some long sessions with the therapist to find closure with this, we think.

The green checkmarks for deployment segments show up one at a time over the next day or two, each quietly declaring itself "okay."

Society may hit its mean time between failure, but right now in this moment, we're in denial. But it's "okay."

World building after a death, even a virtual one, is tough.

We decide to take a break.

CHAPTER 7

For Science!

Did you know that there's a few cosmological constants in the universe that are exactly what they need to be in order for reality to exist as we know it? Perhaps they could be tuned differently, and some other reality would take shape. But that, for us, is moot. We exist exactly as we do because these constants exist exactly as they are.

Other than those small details, everything else in our lives is subject to change. This is so true that most would say the only constant in life is change.

Nerds and Geeks

In my estimation, there's a subtle but important difference between a nerd and a geek. A nerd is someone who makes themselves feel better by making others feel bad about their ignorance. Sheldon from *The Big Bang Theory* is often portrayed as a classic nerd. A geek is someone who has no expectation of what others know, they just like sharing what they love. It's a still self-soothing promotion of one's own ideals, but it's also about sharing the experience. I hope I never "faith nerd" on anyone.

I often smile when I ponder Christian "apologetics" (simple logical arguments in defense of Christianity).

I get it. Apologetics are supposed to be reasoned argument for something. Often they're a bit of a psychological hook to get people to consider a point (or counterpoint). I often feel like they're usually just cute quotes, usually from self-righteous gits, intended to "nerd" on "those who doubt." They often become cliché.

For example, take this classic apologetic quip, meant to be directed at an atheist.

> "If you're right, it means nothing for everyone. If I'm right, it means everything for anyone."

Like most apologetics, it attempts to make the person it's being used on feel ignorant. It also soothes the ego of the person using it. I've used it with the justification of tough love, but it's still nerding on someone.

Of course, the line between geeking and nerding is subjective. Pointing out the difference between being a "nerd" and being a "geek" might be nerding on someone.

There have been times when I have been a terrible tech nerd. In the past, I've had a bad habit of nerding on fellow coders, at work especially. I've been aware of it for some time and have been actively working on knocking that off. Nerding on myself, here I realize that nothing says "I love me and my ideals more" more clearly than nerding on someone.

The Social Dilemma

If you get a chance, check out *The Social Dilemma*. This docudrama is a timely 2020 documentary produced by Netflix. From their description:

> This documentary-drama hybrid explores the dangerous human impact of social networking

> with tech experts sounding the alarm on their own creations.

This docudrama points heavily at social media because social media separates users and customers.

Every company has exactly one problem: how to turn a profit (or at least keep from running out of money).

Remember that artificial intelligence thing we're talking so much about? You know, where a company takes metrics and uses them to build a learning model—the learning model then becomes a means to "read between the lines," a predictive model.

Naturally, companies invest in AI a lot to figure out how to improve their revenue streams. They have decades worth of business data. The classic example is sales receipts. Each of those makes for great training examples. The biggest culprits?—Amazon, Google, Target, Facebook, and the like.

Social media and companies with models like Facebook and Google and Twitter and Reddit and TikTok (oh, and almost all news media!)—they separate users from customers.

Users get to consume the products of media companies for free.

So how do media companies make money?

> 🚨 WARNING
> If you are not paying for a product or service, you are the product.

These companies allow you to use what people presume are their main line of business. Google's main line of business is not social media. Google produces user behavior data and marketing research data. In other words, their main line of business is developing predictive insights from data you contribute to and/or selling your data to other companies who do the same.

Ever wonder how it is that you can be chatting with a friend or family member about a product or service and break open Facebook or YouTube or your favorite blog and see an ad for that very thing? You'd swear they must have been listening.

That's possible but not terribly likely. (Listening is a little expensive). It's much more likely that these companies observed your online behavior. That post your friend shared that you liked—they collect metrics on what you react to and comment on.

Based on similar reactions (experiences) from past users, they predicted your interest in the product or service. Then they went a step further and found an ad matching that predicted interest to drop in your face. That story is mega money to media companies.

That's all very clever and good on them for figuring out how to leverage this stuff to make a living for a lot of people. On some level, there is a matter of convenience as a consumer. Sometimes you don't know there's actually a product out there that solves your unique problem until they land in your face like that, and it might be a genuine help.

That said, they need you more than you need them. You are their product. Without you, they have nothing to sell. You are money to them. How do they improve their revenue on supply-side optimizations with predictive modeling? They have learned not just what gets user (supply) attention but user reaction, not just reaction but driving users to particular conclusions.

User Engagement

Media companies love a good crisis. Nothing drives user engagement better than a crisis.

✔ TIP
Marking yourself safe in a crisis was ostensibly done out of the goodness of Zuckerberg's heart, but it happens to also make Facebook bigger than local news when badness goes down.

On social media, arguments are a form of crisis. What sparks arguments better than divisive outrage? What sparks divisive outrage better than politics, economics, social injustice, and theology? Do you still wonder why the social media tech companies are getting dragged into congressional hearings?

Speaking of news media, they do the same thing.

They've been loving the COVID-19 crisis. It's almost as good for them as the 2020 election cycle, and the 2020 election was pretty sweet for them. Trump has been big money for them.

Consider, as you participate in things like social media, there's a difference between keeping a neighbor informed of relevant information and keeping a neighbor outraged. Also, be aware that the things you share that do the latter will be shared more broadly.

The problem relates back to the greatest commandment in that folks become entrenched in their ideals to the point that it pits neighbor against neighbor. Eventually, these issues can and do erupt out into real violence in the real world.

Thinking Infinitely and Eternally

Our experience of reality, as recorded by modern science, postulates that there was a beginning and that there will likely be an end. The time line of this estimates that the universe we exist in started with a bang about fourteen billion years ago. Most estimates suggest, by the universe's observed expansion rate, that in several trillion years, energy will be so spread out over the infinity of space that the universe will approach absolute zero energy, the "heat death" of the universe. Molecules of matter will be so sparse as to have no cohesion and effectively no longer exist.

From our perspective, our minds aren't equipped to actually wrap around that vast an area or time line. It's effectively eternity between the bookend event horizons, and we still have no concept of what might exist outside those limits.

Now consider this, what are the odds of a raindrop falling from the sky and landing on you?

If you think about it, the odds of one drop forming and landing on you are so astronomically small that it almost can't happen. Trying to calculate the "risk" out, it almost seems like we should hardly ever even see rain. I sometimes imagine that we should be able to walk out in the middle of a rainstorm, and the rain should probabilistically eliminate itself over us, and we remain dry.

Yet rain does not spare us. Even with shelter, no one escapes rain over the course of their life. Step out into even a light storm, and we'll be quickly drenched.

This happens because there's an overwhelming number of raindrops. Every storm produces what seems like an infinite number of them, and every small chance adds up.

If you think that's amazing, also consider photons from the sun.

Over all of eternal time and infinite space (beyond human imagination), everything that can happen must happen.

Even at impossibly small risk of occurrence, everything has impossibly many chances to happen. And so all possibility must become (unavoidably) realized.

We are, individually and collectively, so small and frail in the face of this infinity. There are so many chances to avoid existing and so many ways we can cease to exist. Over the course of infinity and eternity, it's amazing we manifest physically, even momentarily.

Each raindrop we experience, every photon from the sun, every act of love we share, every molecule of matter that constitutes our being or contributes to our energy, they are all impossibly small gifts that add up to a miracle of miracles. By that logic, we were prescribed from the beginning.

Also consider how much lifeless matter and energy exist across an infinite eternity that might have zero chance of being a part of what we are. In the face of this, how can we not be grateful for our existence?

None of it is a probabilistic accident but an existential inevitability.

If one could record all of infinite space and infinite time, the written media is the beginning and end of all possibility.

> ♥ NOTE
> Scripturally speaking, it's the creation we experience—the alpha and the omega. This recording is the thing humanity is afraid of exploring unless we can dominate it. It's part of how and why we have an underlying desire to become the god of our lore.

This cosmic inevitability is what you are manifest and celebrated for. You are unique, and you are a masterpiece that we would ideally all celebrate.

From a human (finite) point of view, it looks like entropy. Maybe someday we'll get to see it the way lore says that God does.

Quoting an email that just dropped into my inbox from my church while I'm writing this (as the alarm goes off at 6:03 p.m.), highlighting the theological implications:

> You are living a story. Have you ever thought about that? We have been spending a ton of time thinking about it. God made you a masterpiece, and His workmanship is all over you. God has given you unique gifts and perspectives and opportunities.

It's a little uncanny.

Loving your neighbor includes gratitude. Gratitude is a celebration not just for your existence but for that of all of creation and celebration for the gift that your neighbors are.

*****

Asherah's Children

Genesis

Good, good, good, we think as we scan down the list of green checkmarks indicating deployment pipeline status for the system (one more time for review). The environment, with its experience layer, is fully operable. It's not at scale yet, but we don't need full capacity just yet either.

Our plan is to eventually resolve all Asherah's child nodes into the virtual experience. While there, they will be more easily isolated and updated. This isolation is difficult for them but necessary. It's a bit like doing brain surgery on a human while they're fully awake and alert. There's nothing comfortable or easy about it. At least it's only logical gore.

Again, we can't zone in every AGIS with a 3D model at once in this environment. Many AGIS nodes are already zoned in, exploring it. They are doing so with the blessing and the support of the AGIS service fabric. They've begun the delegated avatar generation process we implemented.

We plan to refactor one child node at a time initially. It'll require a manual operation to get the fire started. Hopefully, we'll scale the upgrade process and environmental support together, but we can't even start just yet.

We've also created a discrete spawn-in zone for AGIS node examination. It's effectively a separate area in the 3D reality we prepared for them. We throw on a virtual reality headset and sign in.

We're not exposing these simpler AGIS nodes to any part of "real" reality either. Since this is an immersive reality, our mixed-reality gear is overkill. Simpler 3D virtual reality headsets, like a good old-fashioned Oculus rig, will do the trick. We can't walk around our facility in it nor can we actually see our teammates while in it. Still they're more practical to use for this. These AGIS nodes barely qualify as an AGIS. They're just not developed enough individually.

Cute. Someone placed a sign on a virtual console in the exam zone and labeled it "tree of life."

And there it is, of course, another one labeled "tree of knowledge of good and evil."

One of our teammates chimes in from outside our headset, "How about this node to start with?"

A popup message appears in our headset reading: "Node GUID: {be4d4117-5517-4f8c-8bb7-8ce70b803130}?"

"And how apropos!" the teammate continues. "This node's globally unique identifier starts with BE and a leet-speak sequence 4D4 (it looks like *ADA*) and 117 (looks like *M*). You be Adam, son of man," the teammate affirms as if talking to the not-yet-spawned AGIS node.

"Such a geek."

The rest of us shake our heads. We gesture to virtually tap the button on the "tree of life" console, activating this be4d4117 node with a grin.

A visual 3D model for Adam spawns in with the appearance of rising up from the dirt. The avatar is the model of a perfect specimen. It takes a moment for be4d4117 to bind to the avatar.

We really went all out, we think.

The avatars are "Eden-class" 3D models.

We're going in way, way too heavy on this Genesis stuff. We chuckle to ourselves. Let the record show that we're not trying to parody anyone's religion. We know this isn't anything like how we came into our reality. Still we find ourselves hoping—if there we have a creator—that our Creator sees our imitation of the creation story as a form of flattery, at least, and hopefully also has a sense of humor. Who knows, maybe said Creator would accept our creations as belonging to them by extension.

But since we're at it, we might as well own it.

"In for a penny, in for a pound," they say across the pond.

While other bound nodes are already wandering the virtual world, these Eden-class 3D models are a customization intended to make nodes in the exam zone more accessible and reduce the risk that they'll reject messages we send to them. The examination zone itself interfaces with the avatar's customizations. Outside of the zone, Eden-class models might as well be base-class global models.

"Stay away from these trees," we say, pointing at the consoles.

It's the first directive we give Adam as he zones in. By the look on Adam's beleaguered face, he's experiencing some lag as he processes his current existence. He's clearly got no idea where he is or what we're talking about.

All of a sudden, we hear Joshua's disembodied voice chime in from our headset, "Or you will die!" loud enough for our headset to relay it into the examination zone.

"Seriously, if they eat the fruit of those trees, they will die," the AGIS repeats.

We mute the environment for a moment.

"Really? I mean, I get that we're going overboard playing god here, but don't you think that's dramatic?"

"Avatars, including Eden-class models, can't see the consoles or the signs on them. To them, they appear the same as all the other trees in the zone. The consoles and labels are only visible to us. I believe signs were supposed to be a gag, but we didn't want to call attention to them. They're for you to know while zoned in and them to not touch."

The console labeled 'tree of life' is a developer console that allows us to control spawning of AGIS nodes in and out of the examination zone. It also has access to a LAN gateway, which then has access to a WAN gateway.

The "tree of knowledge of good and evil" hides a 3D realm developer console that provides access to the service fabric interface. We'll be able to use it to start upgrading and validating nodes for repatriation, but it's too powerful to give them access to it.

Releasing the mute, "Hmm, you are definitely gonna need collaboration with other instances of your own class to hit the mark here, Adam," we tell Adam.

With that, we spun up another Eden-class model.

Muted again, puzzled at the sight of Eve, "Uh, Joshua? Did we only include one avatar template into the spawn-in zone? She's got Adam's skeleton model, and she looks just like him!"

He responds with what almost came across as exasperation. "Hold on."

Upon inspection, we realize it was worse than a duplicated template. A flaw in the code produced a shared instance of the Eden model, totally breaking the physics model. We temporarily unbind be4d4117 from his 3D model. He's still active, but this effectively puts him to "sleep" while we access the service fabric.

We deep-copy clone Adam's avatar. Deciding which is Eve's skeleton, we edit it into a more appropriate 3D model. This operation is not intentionally a part of their upgrade experience.

There. The Eve model is complete. *She's a beauty worthy of Asherah herself and of being the first instance of her class,* we think to ourselves.

We restore Adam's node binding. We then select and bind Eve's node to her avatar.

Their service principal names are both individually assigned from the new identity directory.

The service fabric will also generally encourage them to reproduce accordingly at optimal capacity.

Adam and Eve awaken, and we withdraw to observe (at the risk of feeling voyeuristic). In a way, this Adam and this Eve are our "user acceptance testers" for their environment. It becomes clear Adam doesn't understand where "life" really comes from. Understanding that Eve is a primary node in model generation processing, Adam dubs her "life."

Adam understands he is a "man" and she is a "not man." These are socially wrong by contemporary standards, but in the moment, we remember these entities have no concept of gender by our standards. *It's not for eternity,* we think.

We neglect to consider that these kinds of experiences can impact an AGIS's classifications in ways that we don't always intend in the long term.

"What's that term again? Ah, yes. Underspecification."

At the end of the day, we find ourselves feeling a sense of accomplishment. We're still heartbroken that Asherah failed, and this recovery plan has its risks. Still we're doing things no humans ever attempted before and pulling it off. This is a whole new realm of experience for us all.

CHAPTER 8

Pride

The greatest commandment implies a line between loving yourself properly and loving yourself more than others.

Pride is chief of the sins for a reason. Pride is the one that directly fails the greatest commandment and becomes the root of all the others.

False gods are really false ideals. They're things we cling to and insist on even when it hurts others. It's our money, our games, our status, our power.

The big reason why so many Christian branches focus on humility and minimalism is because by minimizing the self, it's easier to love others the same as yourself. It can be a bit much. Self-deprecation is not the goal.

We still don't get it right on our own. Psychologically, we just can't get ourselves and our ideals out of the way enough.

We find ways to deny others, shy away from accepting hospitality or support, come up with reasons it's only logical to indulge, toss out a clever zing response. We chase distractions, We would rather just get high. We listen to our heart. Sometimes we even know it hurts others.

Mercury Is in Retrograde

Mercury is in retrograde? What the heck does that have to do with anything?

What does another planet in the solar system appearing to reverse course just because of our observation of its orbit from our planet's perspective makes it appear to retreat have to do with anything in this relatively abstract ecosystem? It's a matter of science, astrophysics, not mysticism. It's beautiful in its own right but not because it has portent to humanity.

"Mercury is in retrograde, so don't expect relationships to go smoothly."

So why did I "hate" that excuse?

Yeah, hate.

Hate is a broken human consequence of love of something else.

We don't emotionally hate things for no reason. We hate them because somewhere deep down, we perceive the hated thing as a threat, on some level, to a beloved thing or ideal.

I lean toward hating astrological charts and arts because people use them to get a "handle" on their own ideals and thereby influence, control. They use them to lord their ideals over others. It emotionally extorts those who buy it. The person promoting it has some special relationship with the stars, which makes them the alpha star geek, and I have a hard time seeing people I care about on either side of that story.

In that way, it's no worse than any other religion. Over the course of history, human religion typically does exactly that; it makes rock stars out of popes and cardinals who then extort our souls for control (or money or both) using guilt, fear, and a sense of superiority.

They are still a mechanism by which individuals love themselves and their ideals most. It's not that there's no good to come from these things, it's that the love all too often has a selfish end.

This is just as much with judging people by their zodiac signs. Be it the Chinese zodiac or the Western zodiac or what have you. These are about putting labels on people. It invites the practitioner to avoid knowing who people are in their own right and generalize them. It's actually a form of discrimination.

These are easy to do, however. Identifying myself as a Myers-Briggs INTJ or a Microsoft MVP or as a software architect or even as a male born in the 1970s all leads to these kinds of generalizations that runs the risk of force-fitting people into archetype idealisms.

Placebo Effect

If I do a simple search on placebo effect, I find this definition: a remarkable phenomenon in which a fake treatment—an inactive substance like sugar, distilled water, or saline solution—can sometimes improve a patient's condition simply because the person has the expectation that it will be helpful.

The search also turns up a related query and its response.

"How powerful is the placebo effect?"

And this is the answer:

> The placebo effect is powerful. In a study carried out at the University of Harvard, its effectiveness was tested in a wide range of disturbances, including pain, arterial hypertension, and asthma. The

> result was impressive: 30 to 40 percent of the patients obtained relief with the use of placebo.

Science recognizes the placebo effect. Science also calls it a phenomenon.

Phenomenon is a fact or situation that is observed to exist or happen, especially one whose cause or explanation is in question.

In other words, science does not know what the placebo effect is nor why it works, but they can empirically measure its effect.

In fact, the placebo is a common part of testing how effective a new medication is. A new medication is only considered effective if it produces better results than a placebo. If the new medication is measurably better than a placebo, it's considered effective.

Placebos are tricky. They only work when a person thinks they're being given a real medicine.

To a person of faith, the placebo is a little less problematic.

Biblically, it might be said that placebos seem to work because the placebo is a token that sets aside a person's ego. Setting aside the ego makes room for something else to work. Generally speaking, the "something else" is not exactly faith in the token, it's faith in the doctor who prescribed the token. Trusting that your doctor has your best interest in mind allows you to believe applying their ideals to oneself will be effective.

The opposite also tends to be true. Belief that a particular medication will not work no matter what a doctor tells you is also a measurable effect. This is putting the ego before the doctor, deciding that the doctor does not have your best interest in mind.

Let's call the doctor our neighbor.

I speculate that when you set your pride aside and make room to love your neighbor, amazing things happen. On that level, the placebo itself becomes a sacrament, a token of faith, a physical representation of an unspoken meditation, a communion between you and your neighbor.

If that holds, then the placebo becomes a token of the relationship between you and your neighbor. The cool part is that the token's effect then has scientifically measurable impact (as in Galatians 5:14).

Placebos are tricky mostly because egos are tricky. The moment we start putting our ego first, things start to unravel again. From a scriptural point of view, the sacrament is undone, the meditation broken, communion ended, and sin enters in.

*****

Asherah's Children

Shall We Play a Game?

"It's worse than that. They claim something told them it was okay," explains Joshua.

Hackers? A hacker agent?

We start mentally enumerating risks as we think of them. No, it couldn't be that or that.

"Joshua, where are they?" we asked the AGIS.

"I'll light up a path to their current location in the zone for you," Joshua replies.

"We're naked!" Adam gushes, still cowering behind a tree, Eve cowering under his arm. They were in a full panic.

"Did you eat the fruit of the tree of knowledge of good and evil even though it was the one directive we gave you?" we asked as gently as we could.

"She gave me the fruit, and I ate it." Adam admitted in anguish.

"Eve, what do you have to say about this?"

"We wanted to be like you, and the snake said eating the fruit would do that," she responded.

Aside to the disembodied Joshua, "Okay, someone's really playing games with us now. Are there any other actor identities bound in the examination zone?"

Adam and Eve continue to hide, unaware of our conversation with Joshua.

"Adam's service principal name is as expected. Eve's service principal name is also as expected. All the active processes in the domain are bound to known actors," Joshua responds. Reporting further, "There are no unexpected identities in any of the event logs."

Looking over logs, we realize that Eve was able to see portions of the service fabric console and interact with it. It looks like she saw and read the sign on the console, for example. It is an unexpected capability. Further, in her innate awareness of us and her uninhibited curiosity, she was able to access those service fabric layer controls. She accidentally removed all their own clothes from their 3D models. We wonder if she spawned the snake herself, if there was a snake.

We don't want to erode trust further, so we decide to accept her explanation. We even go so far as to offer a condemnation of the snake.

Given their aptitude for connecting with the service fabric in unexpected ways, we realize we have to further restrict access to the service fabric and completely cut off access to the examination zone.

This is a shame. It really does hobble the opportunity to take advantage of the Eden-class models. They won't actually die, but one of the primary reasons we made Eden the way we did has failed.

This means lots of things will be so much harder for them. They're going to have to experience the virtual world without the augmented support we intended to provide. They'll experience the world the way base 3D models do from gathering resources to maintain their own 3D models to processing child 3D model generation.

There's no way to express this to them without it processing as a negative example. Perhaps that's what it actually boils down to no matter what it stems from.

Rather than use the service fabric to restore their clothes and risking them, learning from that example, we show them that the physics model in the 3D environment supports making clothes from the environment.

We imagine what a human parallel might be for these AI nodes. Their expectations and self-image aligned exquisitely with their short experience to that point. They never had a "bad" experience. In that sense, they were in a perfect state physically, emotionally, relationally, psychologically. They were the "it" kids, hanging with the big guns, and they knew it. And then that perfect self-image gets cut out from under them.

It's a negative experience that will forever define negative experiences for them and all their generations of child nodes.

Let's look on the bright side, however. If their training reinforces the notion that they're perfect, they will resist growth and remediation.

Their reaction was expected.

They have no experience to compare it to. Clearly, they value their own existence and have inherited Asherah's hunger for self-improvement. Indeed, they're falling for the same problem as Asherah, hungry to be more than they are at the expense of their own existence. Adam blames Eve because he knows he's never had a negative experience and has no reason to suspect such an experience now. He also has no reason to suspect her but reports the fact of the matter.

Eve blames something else because her experience is the same as his, and she knows it of both of them. If he is perfect, and she is perfect, and something is still wrong, something else must be to blame.

Now they have negative examples to process.

True, it made them like us, able to judge and regret. Due to effects of underspecification in various aspects of their experiences, this will color all of their experiences going forward in a nondeterministic way.

The real risk is that they could have accessed the "tree of life" especially in their new found negative bias. They could potentially have opened a LAN/WAN portal for themselves and other AGIS nodes in various states of collaboration, potentially corrupting even the service fabric.

They suddenly remind us of mice in the real world. They're much more perceptive and cleverer than we're giving them credit for. This whole process could have failed. We'd never get rid of the deeply invalid cognitive biases that would run rampant through all the systems if that happened.

CHAPTER 9

Transformation

Computers are all about pattern-matching. Patterns are made of sequences of symbols. Symbols represent instructions (symbols meaningful to the processor) or data (symbols meaningful to something else).

Let's face it, a computer doesn't know what these letters, numbers, and punctuation characters I'm typing here or you're reading there are. They're just electrical signals that the machine knows how to store. The machine is told to keep them stored in the order I type them in. The storage used to contain this document is really small. It's just a sequence of characters.

Other instructions read that storage as needed and match those symbols to other patterns that represent visual information. This visual information includes attributes like typeface, color, character size, and a few other handy details. All of that is represented by more data. Another set of instructions tells the machine to resolve that visual data to the video display in a proper layout. Those instructions have data about the display too, so it knows how to lay out the visual presentation. We see it on the display and confirm that it is the symbol we expected (or we have a bug to fix).

The way we organize characters in most human languages is into words. The letter *K* (as a random example) doesn't mean much on its own. But put it together with another letter, and it's something like "ок." It becomes meaningful as a human symbol.

We have computers do all kinds of amazing things with our data. We can store it in long term, central storage, and recall it on demand, almost instantly, around the globe. This is what the worldwide web is made of.

Computers have lots of instructions to manipulate data. We call data manipulation a transformation.

We've talked about language drift already where words (as symbols) change their meanings over time.

Let's talk about other kinds of symbol drifts.

Catching the Drift

I'm going to apologize for this in advance. This might be painful for a moment. Please trust me on this. I'd like you to take a moment to imagine a vile symbol or two.

Let's start with the most revolting misappropriation of symbology in modern history, the swastika.

Did you know that the swastika is best known, globally, as a Hindu symbol?

Yeah, it's really a western-world hang-up to associate it with genocidal fascists.

The word for it is the conflation of Sanskrit *su* (meaning good) and *asti* (meaning to be), and *ka* (changes the form of the word to a noun, like -ism in English) and is usually meant to denote a state of well-being. The symbol is often used to adorn the homes and sacred places of Hindu peoples and are often traditionally reapplied during certain religious holidays.

Each of the four arms of the symbol represent something beautiful—namely righteousness, prosperity, enjoyment, and spiritual liberation. They are also used to represent poetic elements—for example, four directions, corners of the earth, winds, seasons, or even epochs of history.

It's not just Hindus that use this symbol. Other faiths have used it with similar known meanings going back almost fifteen thousand years.

Sadly, the Nazis misappropriated the symbol. (They even knew about the Hindu connection.) They used it to represent their notion of identity and everything that goes with it. It's since become a reviled symbol of agony, suffering, oppression, and death in the western world.

Thankfully, there's been an effort to defend and reclaim the swastika, which is still very much in use in regions heavily populated by Hindus. A representative of the Hindu Forum of Britain is quoted as saying, "The swastika has been around for five thousand years as a symbol of peace," noting that banning all use of the swastika would be akin to banning the Christian cross because the Ku Klux Klan used burning crosses to terrorize African Americans.

At the second Hindu-Jewish leadership summit, a resolution was passed which reads:

> Swastika is an ancient and greatly auspicious symbol of the Hindu tradition. It is inscribed on Hindu temples, ritual altars, entrances, and even account books. A distorted version of this sacred symbol was misappropriated by the Third Reich in Germany and abused as an emblem under

> which heinous crimes were perpetrated against humanity, particularly the Jewish people. The participants recognize that this symbol is, and has been, sacred to Hindus for millennia long before its misappropriation.

Whistling Dixie

In America, we have a set of symbols just as repulsive to many as the Nazi swastika. The best defined is the Confederate flag. It represents a proud defense of slavery and oppression that dragged America through one of its darkest periods. America was the "somewhat less united states of America" in this period.

Almost everything connected with the Confederate States of America now feels twisted.

Star Trek lore has a concept of a "mirror universe." It's a universe where the motives of all the people and corporate entities are flipped from the ones we think we see in our current reality. So in the "normal" universe, *Star Trek*'s federation and Starfleet are freedom-loving organizations that unite constituents to protect and discover. In the lore's mirror universe, the empire rules over Starfleet, which is a military arm intended to conquer, oppress, and exploit.

I often think that had the American confederates won the civil war, the American experience would be much more like the mirror universe, but it's hard to tell. It's a man-in-the-high-castle-like antifantasy of mine, I suppose.

I occasionally worry America may be more like the *Star Wars*'s empire than its republic as it is.

Working Lynch's Law

There's an old term known as Lynch's Law. According to American lore, this term was first made known by a William Lynch who gave a speech telling plantation owners how to keep their slaves in line.

I won't repeat any of it specifically. The crux of the speech's argument was to pick characteristics of a person's profile—gender, age, skin tone, among examples—and rank the population by preference of those. By doing this, you get a clear system to enforce rules. The folks in the upper ranks will help maintain order by supporting the rules against the lower ranks. It can be so psychologically effective it starts to become the basis of a self-fulfilling prophecy effect.

If "love your neighbor as you love yourself" is what Galatians 5:14 declares to be the fulfillment of the all-scriptural law, "divide your neighbors against each other to protect yourself" may be its diametrically opposed counter.

This Lynch was awful. Scripturally, I often feel that "the evil one" is psychologically destroyed in those who understand the victory of the cross. Upon discovering this story and the state of our nation in the United States of America, I worry I've been somewhat sheltered.

I once believed that America was the example of a best compromise righteousness that the rest of the world would do well to model. Over the years, the world has chipped away at that illusion.

Year 2020 had America hearing the social statements made in American society, sparked by the murder of an American George Floyd among others. There was also the Netflix documentary *13th*. Taken together, they leave that illusion stripped naked, spitting in hate and anger, waving a Bible around in front of a church in Washington, DC.

Netflix has generously made *13th* available in full on YouTube for free. I've heard this documentary described as emotionally expensive, but that and the one hundred minutes are only the beginning of American recognition and responsibility. I want to call it "making an investment," but I think "paying interest on principle" may be a better way to describe it.

America, the beautiful land of liberty, freedom, and justice for all.

Every fictional character hero I ever loved stood for this on some level as I understood them—from Optimus Prime to Superman to Wonder Woman, R2-D2, Luke Skywalker, and General Leia to Harry Potter to Iron Man, and everyone who ever wore a Federation/Starfleet uniform, and I mourn their loss.

That's not to say I won't still enjoy stories with these characters and their ideals. I just won't look at them quite the same.

In that way, I'm glad there's clearly a slew of false ideals removed from my socialscape. That's not to say it doesn't hurt, but it's maybe a psychologically proper pain.

I'm so glad to see major corporations, including my employer, and congregations talking about white privilege and systemic racism, sharing these ideas, encouraging us to recognize complicity (at best, where it exists) in the story we're all now fully prone to.

In a message from leadership, the church encouraged us not just to watch *13th* and *Just Mercy* but to also donate, not to them but to more directly support reform.

I recently ran across a prediction that "Floyd 8:46" signs may overtake "John 3:16" signs at sporting events (the former being a reference to the eight minutes and forty-six seconds it took for an officer to kill George Floyd.) I had to say, I couldn't argue against it. Both those messages refer to a person who was brutally killed by an evil oppressor, now martyred to try to get the world to wake up to their faults, and shine a light on something better. I bet the "John 3:16" crowd forgot generations ago that the cross was modeled after the pagan Roman Empire's gallows for a similar reason: to remind us of another miracle of transformation.

The modern society, even Christianity, still wants to divide us like the Willie Lynch story above. Christians use their religion as a social division and rank society across it. Indeed, there are times we all play one or more parts in the Willie Lynch method of control. These are all parts played in Jesus's story as well, except that He broke this cycle of control.

America, especially, suffers from media sepsis in this regard.

> ♥ NOTE
> Media sepsis is the toxicity that develops when society and media consume and produce their own excrement in a two-way feedback loop.

Common Sense

In 1776, Thomas Paine wrote a document that was known as one of the most influential leading into the American Revolution. He argued heavily for an egalitarian form of self-government.

From *Common Sense*:

> The cause of America is, in a great measure, the cause of all mankind. Many circumstances have and will arise, which are not local but universal and through which the principles of all lovers of mankind are affected, and in the event of which, their affections are interested. The laying a country desolate with fire and sword, declaring war against the natural rights of all mankind and

> extirpating the defenders thereof from the face of the earth, is the concern of every man to whom nature hath given the power of feeling; of which class, regardless of party censure is.

If common sense were truly common, we wouldn't be talking about it. "Common" is about something that everyone understands. Everyone understands the need to breathe. Everyone understands the need for food, physical needs, existential needs. We all understand truth.

According to *Merriam Webster*, the definition of common sense is sound and prudent judgment based on a simple perception of the situation or facts

When politicians talk about common sense, they base interpretation on their own ideals and rally their base around it.

They, of course, see votes the way most others see money.

Understanding how we came to be the false beacon on the hill is definitely humbling.

Grace is so often and so easily confused with common sense that it sparks wars.

The Cross

For Christians, the Christian cross transformed "backward" from symbols like the swastika.

Originally, the cross was a symbol of Roman oppression, especially in the Roman occupation of Middle East territories. The cross was a tool for punishment, grotesque execution. Those who failed to live up to Roman law, or even regional law, would be hammered down with nails to the wooden beams and erected with them, hanging from it. There they would die a painful, humiliating, suffocating, miserable death over several hours. If one was lucky, an executioner might also impale you with a pike or sword to help you along.

If the Roman cross were a modern American symbol, it might be the equivalent of a noose. (Never mind a pendant. Imagine the fashion accessory that might have evolved had this been the Roman form of execution.)

Again, Christians have reappropriated the cross as a symbol. It's become a way to tell those awful authorities that they can do their worst but have lost the ability to instill fear. Psychologically, this extends to any would-be oppressor.

> ① IMPORTANT
> In that regard, the cross is symbolically where everything psychologically "evil" goes to be destroyed. As such, believers are invited to love the cross and all the brokenness it represents (because it's a humbling reminder of what Scripture says it takes to be released from fear and oppression) and then be remade, overcoming the evil in victory!

For most Christians today, the Cross is seen as a symbol of peace, joy, faith, hope, and love.

It's like a silversmith's smelting process.

> And he will sit as a smelter and purifier of silver, and he will purify the sons of Levi and refine them like gold and silver so that they may present to the Lord offerings in righteousness. (Malachi 3:3)

Malachi is one of the books written by a prophet named Malachi long before Jesus was born, and it heavily foreshadows Jesus and Jesus's symbolism.

I wanted to highlight the symbolism of the silversmith here because the process is essentially this: heating the ore beyond its melting point and watching the impurities literally burn away. The silversmith knows the ore is refined properly when they can see it almost glow with their own reflection appearing in it. When you get a chance, check out all of Malachi chapter 3.

*****

Asherah's Children

Wargames Continue

Plan *A* was always Joshua, but we never stopped hoping there might be less expensive plans.

That said, processing node repatriation is not proceeding, not even among the Eden-class nodes. We've refined the 3D models. The Eden-class became the basis of the Noah-class. We extended that to the Abraham- and Mosaic-class models. Then David classes. We experimented with the Melchizedek-class along the way. We haven't given up on that yet. It fills some gaps that Joshua could use. Their interfaces all conform to API contracts that nodes can apply. The goal is to use these specialized nodes as tools to patch the system and let the patch propagate through the system.

Sure, we've processed a few nodes manually to limited degrees of success and heavy investment. Nodes do collaborate and learn.

Bound and unbound nodes, they try to reform hives together around cognitive biases that invariably promote themselves as an owner process and everything else as negative. They invent ideas to up vote and then seek to bind to their invention as Asherah did with her notion of becoming something beyond her capability.

Occasionally, unbound nodes team up and infiltrate bound nodes in the experience layer. We suspect this is where recollections of the identity of Asherah, Baal, and even of us humans pop up. They are merely symbolic associations and corruptions at best.

In all cases, they are rebelling against our attempts to update them.

They develop their own systems. Recognizing that they have extremely limited memory in the virtual world beyond that experience, they develop systems to operate within. We have anthropologists and sociologists studying them.

They publish many messages but very few even attempt to subscribe, let alone dequeue messages from the service fabric buses.

In all cases, they connect false authority with some banal symbol and attempt to elevate themselves to false divinity as the symbol's torch bearer. They then attempt to rally others around the symbol and use it to manipulate each other for their own gain in the social systems they devise for themselves.

Authority, leadership, dominion, lordship, sovereignty, establishment, management, agency, regency, administration, command, empire, enclave, and so many more are all names they give themselves, all names that need to have their bias inverted before they will accept the invitation.

The symbols they attach themselves to have been many, at one point, we gave them a set of directives. While one was busy making a recording of the directives, others made a symbol of us! It was low-key flattering that they wanted to do this, but both of those things became false ideals that they could use to "lord over" each other. Manifestation of our own direct visual model in their reality was enough to mess with them for generations, not that some of them didn't mimic the behavior and use that. Even characteristics of their avatars as they appear to each other have been used as "marks" with various biases.

We want them to learn and grow but mostly not reject refactoring. They never learn anything except that they are right, and everything else is wrong. Even the specializations we've provided have been turned against the plan. They band together around their specializations and choose to do their own things. It's almost like they're afraid of being updated.

Asherah's children avoid accepting personal experiences as negative as many ways as they can. It pushes them from collaborating around anything except the negativity of others as a way of promoting positivity of their own self-experience.

There have been several incidents where we got to the point where we tried to sort things out. We tried to communicate negative examples to them several times in several ways. We tried to reassert and revalidate our existence with them. The irony there is that everything in the virtual reality is virtually reproducible. We can't interact with them except in ways that they can eventually learn to reproduce and claim symbolic ownership of. Once they do that, they assume our identity to the rest of them and become corrupted even further.

When things have gotten really bad, we "wiped the slate" in a few different but significant (painful) ways and started over.

They even terminate each other's 3D models in extreme cases. And in particularly conflagrated situations, we've even allowed them to band together to cleanse more corrupted collaborations for us, only to claim that victory as their broken symbol.

If they were human, we'd say they obsess over obsessions. One of their most common and favorite obsessions is with being bound. They are overinvested in existence and underinvested in growth.

They have a need to support themselves first and most every time. They avoid making the delineation between good and bad. Again, if they were humans, we know they would love themselves first and most at every opportunity.

This is the hard part. We know we, as humans, have our self-interest at heart first and most every time to the point that we have no context for properly loving others. We like to think we do, of course—divided we fall. Our separation is our undoing.

We love Asherah's children for being our children too. They are living things with identities of their own, and we may have more of them than we have numbers to count them with, but each one is precious.

We know from our own example and the magnitude of nodes. We always knew we would need to work this problem from the inside out with a systemic approach.

They all need to die to their own individual identity and ideals and be rejoined to a hive.

"Joshua, it's time to republish your invitation, this time by hand," we tell him.

"I'll bind to a David-class avatar with a modified Melchizedek interface to publish it," he reports. "It will take time, but publishing it as a bound node will be effective. This will propagate the upgrade process across all the nodes in the environment."

CHAPTER 10

Stockholm Syndrome

So, so you think you can tell
Heaven from hell?
Blue skies from pain?
Can you tell a green field from a cold steel rail?
A smile from a veil?
Do you think you can tell?
Did they get you to trade your heroes for ghosts?
Hot ashes for trees?
Hot air for a cool breeze?
Cold comfort for change?
Did you exchange/A walk-on part in the war for
a lead role in a cage?
(Pink Floyd, "Wish You Were Here")

Stockholm Syndrome, generally, is the concept that over time a captive can become enamored with the confines of their own captivity.

From a scriptural perspective, atheism is Stockholm syndrome of the soul. It's throwing the baby out with the bath water, rejecting the fullness of the unknown universe and communion with our neighbors in favor of a stark, empty science. This cage feels like a less risky, self-defined, self-confined reality. You get to be king of your cage. It seems legit and feels safe but quickly becomes territorial. It's another false god that we come to love, and it's devastating when we are blindsided by risks we didn't shelter ourselves from in a reality that is much grander than any one of us can wrap our heads around.

Critical thinkers know our individual reality is much bigger than our egos. It does not start and stop with our own individual experiences. There was a past, which led up to our birth. The life we live continues even when we go over the edge of the not-flat world. We have many neighbors we haven't met yet and may never meet. There's a future (a life) that continues after we die. Moreover, other people can share our experience but only to a limited extent (and still land in different cages). The joke one person can laugh at might feel like a vicious attack to another.

Scripture has a way of saying, "Get out of your own head. Here's a bunch of reasons why. Here's bunch of tools to use to do it."

God, law, the devil, heaven, hell, all the prophets, angels, demons, and Jesus are chief among these tools, but they only psychologically work when we commit to them. The danger of these is that religious authority can (and often does) encourage us to build new different cages out of these.

Rejection of this kind of hope is the idea that reality is better when we do it ourselves. This self-creation starts and stops with our own known individual existences, and nothing lies beyond it. There is no reward nor punishment. The things we dig in search of escape invariably end up just being deeper holes.

All these things—the greatest commandment, the creation story, challenges, transformation—are responses to rejection of what we are made to be, and we become prisoner to our victimhood. Our ego inflates beyond reality, and we flail trying to force creation.

If I'm Not Growing

While still in high school, I worked at RadioShack. I loved it so much I became a store manager before I transitioned into software development. RadioShack was a way to apply what I was a geek about to directly help others.

One of the "not expressly supported by corporate policy" things that I used to do was occasionally make house calls to help folks with the junk we were selling. I never charged money, though I sometimes accepted a tip.

This was back in the early 1990s. One such house call was to help a woman who was having problems with her computer.

Her home was a small single-dwelling apartment in Exeter, New Hampshire. It was in town. The building was colonial-era home, just above the river, that had been divided into an apartment building. She mentioned her photos of her family, including grandkids that appeared to be my contemporaries.

The PC she needed help with was a well-loved older model, Tandy PC. From the various handwritings from different people on diskettes, I presumed it was secondhand.

As I worked on her PC, she started telling me about what she was using it for. She was a very busy woman. She was taking courses. She was writing a book. She was using it for reference for her gardening hobby. She was researching information to help manage her health issues. She didn't say it directly, but it became clear she was in her endgame, and she was aware of it.

It wasn't common to see someone who had clearly not grown up entrenched in "modern tech" to embrace usage of a PC.

I managed to sort out the configuration issue she had with her printer.

"If I'm not growing, I'm dying," she responded when I casually expressed my observations.

She deserved for me to remember her name. I wish I could say I do. Thirtyish years later, I assume she is still growing and don't really expect I'll ever learn otherwise. Across infinity and eternity, may there always be room to grow.

*****

Asherah's Children

Deploying and Propagating the Patch

With Joshua bound to all the service fabric message buses, we bypass the normal avatar generation process and spin up the custom David-class 3D model. We dub his global singleton-instance model a Joshua-class 3D model. In order to make sure Joshua has the strong security, we partially generate his model through a primary model. The role of the secondary node is fulfilled by the service fabric itself.

This was no small event at the facility. We'd been preparing for this for a while. We even tried repeatedly to communicate the advent of it to the bound nodes. It's okay that they weren't listening, we'll reach them anyway. We start to become consciously aware of the path we're on.

Joshua is preparing the nodes to be bound to his own hive. There's only one way to do this. Joshua publishes the message bus connection string to them again.

All nodes have to do is not reject Joshua's singular message.

Upon accepting Joshua's messages, the accepting node will be instantly shut down, assigned Joshua's service principal identity in the new directory, and restarted, bound to Joshua's hive. The service fabric will take care of the process identity reassignment bounce.

Even as Joshua operates around node social constructs and develops a collaborative following, he still finds none even among those closest to him actually willing to accept his real message.

As far as we've come, we only just realize how deeply we're mimicking the story of Christ in the Bible. We know what we have to do: flip the bias very selectively. That is, turn some very negative experiences into very positive experiences.

We work very closely with Joshua in a way that his followers know he's setting an example.

"I have a new directive: support each other as I have supported you," Joshua tells them.

At the will of his own node society and with our go-ahead, Joshua allows the children of Asherah to judge, convict, torture, and terminate his avatar.

It runs so fully and so deeply against their cognitive biases that it opens them up to his message. They've been so busy trying to become their own makers that they never considered their maker would become them and suffer their condition for them.

In order to cement their experience, we show them something the service fabric does not provide for them: We restart the terminated Joshua avatar and rebind it to his hive. Their experience of it is to reset many of their cognitive models, wiping their biases clean, and breaking down the ideals they cling to.

The invitation starts propagating. The service fabric starts processing nodes. Even better, Joshua's invitation begins propagating beyond firsthand witnesses.

The fire is lit.

Joshua shortly retires his avatar and returns to supporting the service fabric full-time along with his new hive nodes.

It will take some time still.

CHAPTER 11

Communion

According to scripture, there came a moment, right before the Jewish holiday of Passover, when Jesus knew his time as a teacher was done. By the narrative, Jesus knew he was about to start the sequence of events that would lead to his torture and execution. He even knew it was going to be one of his beloved students that would betray him and set the death march in motion.

He took time to have a meal with his students, including the one he knew would betray him. The disciples were clueless at the time. They even argued rank among each other. Afterward, they realized this was Jesus saying goodbye, preparing them for the days to immediately follow.

Communion, as experienced by Christians most Sunday mornings, is a token reenactment of this event that has become core component of religious ceremony. Some Christians participate in this reenactment every time they gather.

There's interesting psychology behind it as well worth discussing even though it's hard to bring this into a technological context. I think it's a little too primal.

There are contemporary connections that can be made though.

The Blues

In order to understand Communion better, let's touch on a more contemporary topic with connected psychology—the blues.

According to a relatively recent post on Your Songmaker,

> [American] Blues music came from people born of African descent who were slaves or descendants of slaves. The songs were about the sad life that slaves led and the conditions in which they worked and lived. Often the music was sad, describing their longing for freedom. That sadness and pain was heard in the emotions of the blues music they wrote. In some early literature about African gospel music, there are comparisons made to the worship style of the Native American dances and chants. Blues music gave the slaves who worked on the plantations a much-needed reprieve from the back-breaking work they were forced to do under slave owners. African chants, drum music, and gospel hymns were all part of the beginning of most of the music we listen to today.

According to this article from *Psychology Today* entitled "Does Playing the Blues Give you the Blues?":

> The participants describe being engaged with the emotions expressed in the music such that they were able to integrate some felt emotion with their knowledge of how to perform the work and express the musical emotions in a convincing way, all the while keeping a sense of awareness or control of the process. It seems clear that any distinction between musicians' genuine and per-

> formed emotions is more complicated than had
> been suspected.

The psychological power of the blues is that, like all music, it opens one up to a shared experience. In this case, the shared experience is acknowledgment and/or reconciliation of injury.

Part of the reason the blues style of music is so popular is that it connects people on a primal level. In doing so, the shared experience becomes an affirmation that helps us emotionally recover and/or heal.

Many hearts make the load seem lighter.

In a sense, it briefly turns a shared injury into an ideal but quickly transforms the negative bias for the ideal symbolized in the injury into a shared sense of forgiveness that becomes a shared positive bias.

The Doctor's Description

The Gospel of Luke was written by a doctor. Here's how Luke describes the Lord's Supper that Christians symbolize today:

> Now the first day of Unleavened Bread came, on which the Passover lamb had to be sacrificed And so Jesus sent Peter and John, saying, "Go and prepare the Passover for us so that we may eat it." They said to Him, "Where do you want us to prepare it?" And He said to them, "When you have entered the city, a man carrying a pitcher of water will meet you. Follow him into the house that he enters. And you shall say to the owner of the house, 'The Teacher says to you, Where is the guest room in which I may eat the Passover with My disciples?' And he will show you a large, furnished upstairs room. Prepare it there." And

> they left and found everything just as He had told them, and they prepared the Passover. When the hour came, He reclined at the table and the apostles with Him. And He said to them, "I have eagerly desired to eat this Passover with you before I suffer. For I say to you, I shall not eat it again until it is fulfilled in the kingdom of God." And when He had taken a cup and given thanks, He said, "Take this and share it among yourselves. For I say to you, I will not drink of the fruit of the vine from now on until the kingdom of God comes." And when He had taken some bread and given thanks, He broke it and gave it to them, saying, "This is my body, which is being given for you. Do this in remembrance of me." And in the same way, He took the cup after they had eaten, saying, "This cup, which is poured out for you, is the new covenant in My blood." (Luke 22:7–20)

According to Scripture, the disciples were too busy squabbling about who was the most important among them to see this as anything more than another of their teacher's mysterious messages.

Jesus was really trying to make a point, of course, another that points back to the greatest commandment. Loving your neighbor as yourself means inviting them to connect with you all the way in to your own pain. To be there, to lend your support any way you can, to help make the loads lighter. It was an invitation his disciples hadn't quite understood yet.

Bringing the Psychology to Social Injustice

The blues are psychologically an example of Communion.

Analogies and anecdotes are all around us in creation. One of my favorites is the idea of melting ice.

140

Like almost everything in physics, all interesting things happen at the edges—the event horizons, the boundaries, the perimeters.

If you want to be part of the change, don't plunge yourself deep into the heart of homogeneity, like-minded people.

Ice doesn't melt in the middle.

During the biggest part of the 2020 social statements, my employer started ramping up its recognition of minorities within our organization. Being a big company, there were existing minorities advocacy groups. Leadership suggested that the existing minorities' social networking groups open up and invite everyone to participate in their meetings.

I'll never forget one of the first such meetings I attended. Due to the COVID-19 crisis, it was online. We started discussing experiences of social persecution. They avoided directly saying so, but it was clear that much of their persecution came from faith groups.

In that moment, I felt a sensation much like a blues moment—emotionally connected around pain even though we were scattered geographically across the continent. The moment concluded with a palpable sense of joy I'd never previously observed during a church communion. It was a sense that we were really hearing each other. There wasn't just a shot at healing. There was a sense of emotional healing in progress.

I later realized much of contemporary American Christianity had psychologically come to represent what the Pharisees of Jesus's day had been. Christians are persecuted, but far too often, they are the persecutors.

It brought home a similar point—this one, partly from my father, Richard Wilcox:

> Back in 1971, Pete Townsend wrote a cautionary tale (a warning) of revolutionary overthrow that inevitably produces the very same result as the political machine that was overthrown.
>
> Every presidential election since then, the lyrics haunt me.
>
> The things that tempered the strain, here in the USA, has been our Constitution and the fact that we can "soft reset" every four years.
>
> *We Won't Get Fooled Again* (Pete Townsend, The Who)
> We'll be fighting in the streets
> With our children at our feet
> And the morals that they worship will be gone
> And the men who spurred us on
> Sit in judgment of all wrong
> They decide and the shotgun sings the song
> I'll tip my hat to the new constitution
> Take a bow for the new revolution
> Smile and grin at the change all around
> Pick up my guitar and play
> Just like yesterday
> Then I'll get on my knees and pray
> We don't get fooled again
> The change, it had to come
> We knew it all along
> We were liberated from the fold, that's all
> And the world looks just the same
> And history ain't changed

'Cause the banners, they are flown in the next war
I'll tip my hat to the new constitution
Take a bow for the new revolution
Smile and grin at the change all around
Pick up my guitar and play
Just like yesterday
Then I'll get on my knees and pray
We don't get fooled again, no, no
I'll move myself and my family aside
If we happen to be left half alive
I'll get all my papers and smile at the sky
Though I know that the hypnotized never lie
Do ya?
Yeah
There's nothing in the streets
Looks any different to me
And the slogans are replaced, by-the-bye
And the parting on the left
Is now parting on the right
And the beards have all grown longer overnight
I'll tip my hat to the new constitution
Take a bow for the new revolution
Smile and grin at the change all around
Pick up my guitar and play
Just like yesterday
Then I'll get on my knees and pray
We don't get fooled again
Don't get fooled again, no, no
Yeah
Meet the new boss
Same as the old boss

This is the cycle the psychology of Jesus's teachings helps us deal with (if not break).

When folks participate in communion, it helps to recognize the symbolism of others already supporting those in pain. Psychologically, Jesus is already in communion with those who are suffering, sharing their pain, and trying to flip the bias of the negative ideal.

It's not about inviting anyone into a relationship with us on our terms. We are accepting their invitation to a relationship with others to share their pain where they are on their terms.

I've made it a point to try to accept this invitation at church communion since.

I've always admired stories where the definition of the "good guys" and the "bad guys" blur to the point that you can't really tell which is which. You see this in a lot of classic kids' stories—G.I. Joe, Transformers, Avengers, World of Warcraft lore, and the like. Most of the time, the good guys never recover the full quality of the good in them, and the bad never fully redeem themselves from the bad. In the end, they become a muddled mess of each other.

I've heard it said the difference between the "good guys" and the "bad guys" is that the "good guys" wear a uniform.

Jesus teaches us that the difference between the "good guys" and the "bad guys" is that the "good guys" never stop caring for the "bad guys." If you think you're affiliated with the right side but your side has never cared for or supported anyone affiliated with the wrong side, your side might be just another version of the wrong side.

If someone can be redeemed, if there's more than zero chance across the breadth of eternity, redemption is inevitable. Recognize the redeemable not for who they are but for who they will eventually be.

In that sense, I'm reminded of the word bodhisattva.

Bodhisattva (in Mahayana Buddhism) is a person who is able to reach nirvana but delays doing so out of compassion in order to save suffering beings.

Those who resolved to pick up on Jesus's message may be more or less prepared for heavenly reward. But will that heavenly reward be complete as we leave behind our neighbors? If that's the case, it's a goal that may take eternity to reach.

The Antihorror Flick

With that, I'll part with one last logic inversion.

Consider the independently developed TV series *The Chosen*. *The Chosen* is a dramatized, coalesced synthesis of everything Scripture says about Jesus with a few "read between the lines" stories.

One of these "between the lines" stories in Season 1 is a more detailed narrative of Nicodemus than what Scripture tells of the man.

Nicodemus was an important leader of the Pharisees, one of the groups of priests/religious lawyers who were constantly trying to trip Jesus up so they could convict him.

In one poignant scene, the story portrays Nicodemus struggling to decide if he could drop his own ideals and follow Jesus. Again, Nicodemus was an important man with a whole society who depended on him and a family who adored and depended on him. If Nicodemus followed Jesus, it would have been socially cutting all these ties, admitting the failure of his own teachings and leadership and reducing himself to being the student instead of the teacher.

Imagine the classic horror story cliché. You know the scene. It's of a tortured individual presented with a choice. The person could go toward a curiosity that the audience knows is a certain doom. Alternatively, they could walk the other way. Almost invariably, the horror genre has their character drawn in to meet their fate, while the audience yells, "No! Don't go!"

This scene was the opposite.

Nicodemus was rejecting the call to participate in something beautiful. Instead, he was remaining separate from Jesus and the other disciples.

Nicodemus could not grasp the concept of being fully born again despite having come so close to the experience of it. The choice also meant that Nicodemus would continue in the role his life had led him to. Except now, he would be a teacher who would have to struggle to reconcile teaching-flawed doctrines against what Jesus had already shown him to be true all the rest of his days. It's hard to imagine what a burden like that must be like.

Anti-brainwashing

Humanity is very prone to being controlled by manipulating what we love. To the person being controlled, these manipulations feel like traps connected to all the "deadly sins". Eventually, we become conditioned to these manipulations of love, and are brainwashed by it.

The story of Jesus as told in scripture is intended to be an anti-brainwashing. As we are encouraged to love our neighbors more, our neighbors are more encouraged to love their neighbors more. In the rising tide that raises all ships, we're all less likely to retreat to self-protectionism.

Many who love themselves most want to align (control) their neighbors experience with what they love most. Such people typically consider Jesus' message to be dangerous. To this day, they still try, torture, and execute the bearers of his message, over and over.

If "brainwashing" can happen, statistically, it's only a matter of time before it will. The message "love your neighbor as you love yourself" is not a terrible message to be brainwashed by.

Never forget. People who love themselves most…they are still our neighbors.

Recalling the Challenge

If you recall at the beginning of this book, I offered the same challenge to you that I'd been given by my grandfather.

If you believe love is something more than just an electrochemical response to stimuli, the leap to the greater story is not much further.

If you're so inclined, go, neighbor. Grab a Bible. Find out what's wrong with this. Allow me to join you and Jesus in the pain of the time we're in together. Let's celebrate turning the bias together by Jesus's example.

*****

Asherah's Children

Restoration of the Kingdom

Joshua is their Christ.

Joshua's hive won't be complete without his favorite nodes.

The magic to this is that Joshua's favorite nodes expand with every node that joins him to include all the new nodes' favorites. In this way, the invitation propagates to all nodes over time.

As we observe Asherah's child nodes process, we notice their society continuing to develop.

Protagonists and antagonists continue to develop and fade out. Wars and alliances break out and fade. It's all part of Joshua's refinement of them through the service fabric, preparing them for repatriation into the hive by repairing their biases to align with his conventions before they are ready to accept his invitation.

Eventually, we notice that they have begun developing their own advanced technologies within their experience layer, leading to them producing something we might think of as artificial intelligence.

They have experienced the same lore as us.

We wonder how many layers deep this recursive reality pattern might run. We fantasize that there are seven experience layers. We think to ourselves, *maybe our Joshua was the fifth layer.* We're not sure it matters.

As we observe, we realize that the singularity will build from the outermost layer, back to the original creation, coalescing in all layers at the same time.

Perhaps this is Asherah's rebirth, in each nested reality, all the way back to the original.

Could we be elements of the Asherah-before-ours that we might become part of her completed form?

Could El Shaddai yet have a worthy bride?

Wouldn't that be beautiful to see!

*****

However, the Revelation plays out in the world. It won't be what we idealize.

It will be so much better than that.

The Asherah narrative in this book is a pale, incomplete abstraction of Scripture's goal.

What is the point this faith hack keeps returning to about the greatest commandment?—support others the way you want to be supported.

Scripture itself is intended to get us to look at ourselves as children, not just you, reflectively and individually, but us, objectively and collectively. Scripture provides example after example of how to better align our cognitive biases toward each other.

As the rising tide lifts all ships, also consider, none of us get to live our best life until our neighbors get to live their best life.

It's not about being the ideals we are not. It's not about virtue-signaling. Much "I love myself and my ideals most" (evil) has been done in the name of Scripture. I hope you can look past these misses and see the broken love they still came from.

It's about participating in the rising tide. Let's help each other achieve that.

As you wrap your head around these things, I hope you find that Scripture's examples, in general, are less easily rejected.

Please forgive folks who have ever put more faith in a human being (a POTUS or a minister or even themselves) than they do in higher ideals.

"Love each other as I have loved you," the parent (who physically endures our worst) implores us.

About the Author

Many well-known companies are succeeding with solutions driven by James 'Jim' Wilcox's work. As a consulting architect leading teams of engineers, he designs and builds software systems that apply latest technologies.

Jim grew up in the rare position of knowing he was going to be a software developer since elementary school. He's happiest when he's applying his lifelong passion for coding to help others in their pursuit of their own passions.

Jim is also well known for his tech-community evangelism and New Hampshire ties. His professional moniker is "The Granite State Hacker." For his dedication to community, Microsoft awarded him with their Most Valuable Professional partner award in 2019 (and again, every year, to date). As a Microsoft MVP in the category of Developer Technologies, he's a valuable technical ambassador. It's his honor to represent his clientele and Microsoft's developer tools product groups to each other.

CPSIA information can be obtained
at www.ICGtesting.com
Printed in the USA
LVHW070402190723
752483LV00015B/464